British Folk Art

Robert Mills

Contents

'Joni Was Dancing'

Staffordshire Bear Jug exhibited at the Festival of Britain in 1951 (See Chapter 4)

Harvest Jug from Barnstaple, Devon, Dated 1741 and inscribed 'Drane by me Thomas Stonman June 27 / Made by me Edward Reed'. The decoration includes the royal arms with lion and unicorn, a man and woman amongst trees and flowers, a stag hunt and a drinking rhyme. 34.1 cms. C1-02.

# Chapter 1 - Introduction

Trying to define Folk Art is like trying to come up with a definition for jazz – it means different things to different people. A quick burst of *The Wild Rover* followed by *Sympathy for the Devil* might suitably illustrate the difficulties involved. Both are popular songs but they are streets apart in structure, meaning and execution. It is the same with *folk* and *fine* art objects. In Britain we do not have an easily recognisable folk style; things would be a lot easier if we had an equivalent of, for example, Australian Aboriginal art.
Perhaps a short fiction will illustrate the problem: A piece of carved wood is bought by a casual collector/dealer at a car boot sale, the vendor describes it as 'a bit of country craft'. The purchaser decides to sell it online at eBay, described as 'a naïve English Popular Art carving'. It is snapped up by a folk art collector who recognises it as an 18th century stay busk. He sells it on at a major auction room, described as 'a unique example of a folk art love token'. The purchaser is a folk art museum who proudly display it as a fine example of British Peasant Art.

There is no generally accepted exact definition of folk art. It is appreciated and identified under a variety of different names – peasant art, naïve art, country craft and so on. With a little practice it is not too difficult to recognise. Anyone with even a slight interest would say that the North Devon harvest jug illustrated on the opposite page is folk art but that this teapot is not.

20th century Lorna Bailey teapot. 18 cms. C1-01.

The term tends to be most often used on small articles, up to perhaps the size of a Windsor chair. A broad definition could include performance folk arts such as dance (for example Morris and Maypole dancing), theatre (Mummer and Miracle plays), music (folk singing, campanology), children's playground games and performance oddities such as gurning. However the size of an object does not necessarily exclude it from the folk art genre. Sizeable pieces of furniture (e.g. Welsh dressers), buildings and items of transport are also part of this tradition along with large scale works such as hill carvings (the Cerne Abbas Giant and the White Horse at Uffington). Folk art is not necessarily permanent; it includes transient creations such as crop circles, topiary, snowmen, scarecrows, tattoos and decorated foodstuffs.

This book looks at objects created in Britain that conform to the generally accepted view of folk art. This includes ceramics, paintings, sculptures, and day-to-day objects with applied decoration. Most of these objects were produced prior to the end of World War II. As well as celebrating these objects I look at the creation of a commercial market from an art form that was originally created for pleasure and entertainment only. Other authors have discussed the difference between hand-produced and machine-produced folk art and between items produced in different parts of Britain. Some have taken a political view, focusing on how folk art reflects social class and struggle. This book focuses on the objects and the difference between commercial and amateur work.

Inevitably the objects featured in the following pages represent a personal selection. My preference is for quirky and more personal objects rather than those pieces that someone with a more 'interior designer' approach might choose.

My thanks go to all of the contributors (listed in Appendix 6) who have helped this book into existence, and to those who have provided information and images solely out of their love of the subject. I would be interested to receive any suggested corrections or additions by email (see Appendix 7). I may even get around to producing a second edition.

Where dimensions are given for the objects pictured they are for the largest dimension, be it height, length or depth, and are in centimetres. For group photographs the largest object is sized. Photograph credits and general references appear in the form Cn-nn and Rn-nn and are listed in Appendix 1.

Bob Mills
October 2011

An 18th century English nutcracker in the form of a man with braided cap.
13.8 cms. C1-01.

Late 19th/early 20th century oak plaque with
country saying. 19.5 cms. C2-03.

 # Chapter 2 - Amateur Folk Art

As already mentioned, a reliable definition of Folk Art is elusive. Type 'folk art' into an internet search engine or online auction site and you will get more results than can be easily interpreted or absorbed. Different authorities provide different formal definitions of the term (some are listed in Appendix 4). The Oxford English Dictionary contains references to Folk dating back to c.1000 AD but their earliest reference to Folk Art is in 1921 (R2-01). This reference is in an article about Czechoslovakian folk art by Prof. Karel Chotek (curator of the Ethnographical Museum, Prague) and it *uses* rather than defines the term; there must surely be earlier printed references.

Accepting that Folk-craft is synonymous with Folk Art (Appendix 5 lists other related terms), the Oxford English Dictionary quotes this limited reference in 1884 : 'Folk-craft, corresponding to the study of art and industry' (R2-02). Having said this, Folk-craft can be interpreted as the ability to do a workman-like job whereas folk art suggests some attempt to lift an object out of the ordinary.

Earlier references which might appear to be relevant are not. For example works such as *Observations on Popular Antiquities* (R2-03) originally published in 1777 documents ceremonies and customs rather than popular antiquities as we might understand them. A book published in 1868 by Herbert Byng Hall called *The Adventures of a Bric-a-Brac Hunter* is dedicated to a European Grand Tour looking for high-end ceramics rather than for bric-a-brac as we might now use the term. So folk art as a descriptive term is probably a twentieth century invention. The etymology of the expression is straightforward: 'Folk' is related to 'country folk' with connotations of a rural life, the common people and the workers; its source is probably the German *volk* meaning people or nation. 'Art' adds a non-functional dimension to give us the Art of the Common People.

Any type of object can qualify as folk art – it does not have to be (and often is not) something produced solely to be admired. It exists as applied art in everyday objects such as knives, forks and crockery as well as in paintings and sculptures. Utilitarian objects such as clothes and tools were raised above the normal with the addition of decoration and dedications. It is this decoration greater than is necessary for their useful purpose that characterises folk art objects.

There is a category of item that some authors (R2-04) consider folk art but which should rather be considered folk craft. These are typically pieces that are aesthetically pleasing but have no attempt at adornment or uniqueness of form that might lift them into the 'art' category. They include items such as woven baskets, rushlight nips, riddleboards and many pieces of straightforward treen (small wooden objects, literally, 'of the tree').

These pieces are aesthetically pleasing because of a simplicity of form and perfection for intended purpose, but they are not folk art. Years of effortlessly handling tools and raw materials did give rise to a certain unconscious artistry which is often displayed to effect in treen objects; however artistry must be conscious to be called art.

Three 19th century plumbers turnpins (foreground), used to bell out the end of pipes and two hatmakers straw splitters (background) all of pleasing but functional rather than artistic form.
9 cms. C2-03.

The effort involved in turning a functional object into a folk art object was sometimes minimal. The addition of a heart-shaped cutout on the backboard of this 18th century elm candlebox lifts it immeasurably.
50 cms. C2-03.

In many cases the decision to add ornament to a basic object was no more than pride in workmanship and a

Late 18th century apple corer. 15 cms. C2-03.

desire to lift something out of the ordinary.

This apple corer would have worked equally efficiently without the addition of caged balls and chip carved decoration but its maker had the time and inclination to create an interesting piece of amateur folk art.

The area between folk craft and art is occupied by the few wonderful pieces where form and function are combined with the original properties of the material to produce something which interprets the object more sculpturally than is necessary for function.

This c.1800 three-legged dog toasting fork admirably demonstrates this point. We will never know whether the creator went looking for a piece of wood that would lend itself to this creation or whether the form of this piece of wood suggested the sculpture. In either case it is a wonderfully naïve and unique piece of functional and very probably amateur folk art when compared with the contemporary but purely functional piece overleaf.

Figural dog toasting fork. c.1800. 48 cms. C2-01.

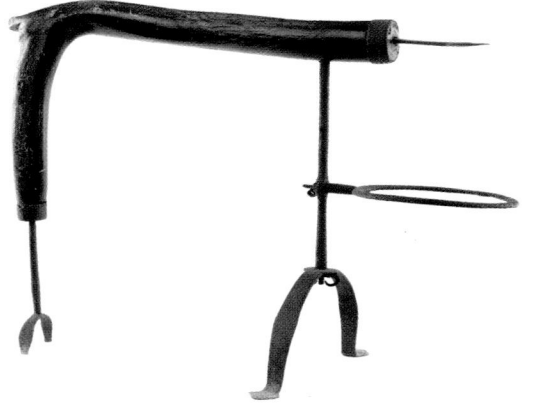

Non-figural toasting dog, elm and iron, contemporary with the sculptural 'dog' version. C2-02.

Amateur folk art has a basic human person-to-person appeal; no knowledge of the fine arts or of any complex iconography is necessary to appreciate it. It is usually anonymous and it talks at a basic level with easily identified representations, images and interpretations. It is often inseparable from a sense of nostalgia and a yearning for the perceived simplistic lifestyle and pleasures of previous times. It is immediate, unsubtle, one-off, naïve and often very charming. If the subject of a piece was real rather than imaginary, the intention of folk art was to reproduce an accurate likeness; lack of training and the 'innocent eye' lead to very honest results. Folk art reflects traditional values; it rarely attempts to introduce new ideas or to make political points.

There is some truth in saying that 'children's art is the true seed of folk art' (R2-05). The expressions of emotion that children put into their creations combined with their relentless observation is present in the best folk art, regardless of medium. Childrens art, such as that found on samplers, often qualifies as folk art.

A basic and most widely-accepted characteristic of folk art is that it is not Art in the Fine Art sense. It is vernacular art, part of an established tradition, breaking few artistic boundaries, often involving traditional crafts and using established styles and techniques. It is produced by people with no formal training in Art who are attempting to produce images and objects for their own sake rather than representations with more than one level of interpretation. Little attempt is made to depict higher ideas or ideals other than perhaps a dedication to a lover or presentation of religious iconography.

Amateur folk art objects were usually made for personal use or for a friend or family member (wife, sweetheart or child) rather than for sale for a profit. They were made with sincerity, often as a conscious expression of affection or admiration. Few amateur folk art pieces were intended for a wide audience, they were made to impress one, or at most a small group of people. Little commercial value was attributed to them when they were produced.

It is difficult to define the term folk art without including the word naïve. It is usually the result of a single craftsman sitting down one day and deciding to add 'a little more' to the object being made. He will have worked out almost entirely for himself how to handle the decoration he wants to apply (sometimes consciously or subconsciously including references to motifs from his rural history) and his efforts are usually considered, not hurriedly dashed out to a pre-conceived design. Images of humans, animals, birds and nature are usually naïve if not childlike.

It is often the irregularities in amateur work that gives it its charm – a spelling mistake, irregular character spacing, depiction of an animal obviously trying to represent real life but looking more mythical than real.

Many of these objects have little to do with western life in the 21st century; the very purpose of many of them is now redundant. For instance the requirement for personalised apple corers used by people lacking sufficient teeth to bite into an apple has disappeared. Because of this distance the connection with the past provided by folk art objects is much stronger than with many other antiques. They are personal art, transported directly from the individual creator to you as the owner or viewer. They often carry the patina and sometimes damage that show they have been used and loved over a long period of time. This acquisition of wear and patina adds greatly to their charm. Treen objects, in particular, exhibit these qualities and collectors appreciate a worn surface with the deep patina that comes from years of handling. Signs of natural wear, traces of original paint, verdigris and a lack of modern restoration are all valued.

The authors Marx and Lambert (R2-06) proposed a very wide definition of folk art which included items such as 19th century broadside newspapers and mass-produced chapbooks. These items are really the products of commerce and would never have been made as one-off gifts or souvenirs. They are not rooted in domestic life and do not therefore qualify for the title folk art. Part of the attraction of amateur folk art is the degree of naïve 'oddness' and apparent lack of purpose in the objects that have been produced; this 19th century model of a coffin carries no inscription, it is just a strange reminder of our mortality - a *memento mori*:

19th century model coffin with body. 16 cms. C2-03.

Folk Artists were non-academic, untrained and only indirectly influenced by fine art; most creators did not consider themselves Artists. What they produced were vigorous vernacular artefacts not examples of sophisticated, articulate fine art. Intellectual analysis of folk art does not usually produce rewards. It does not grow on you once you have analysed its hidden meaning, you either immediately connect with it or discard it as of no interest. It is usually all the better for having been designed and made by the same man, carrying no baggage of formal training.

Perspective, if attempted at all in folk art paintings, does not conform to Brunelleschi's rules. Paintings are flat and features are out of scale. It is an honest art form, unpretentious despite ranging from the barely considered to the accurately planned.

Woman Mounting Donkey, c. 1850,
unknown amateur painter.
In attempting to mount the donkey the
woman has hitched her skirts on the
saddle and given the surprised animal a
view of her behind.
24 cms. C2-03.

Borrowing a quotation from Jeremy Deller (who organised an exhibition featuring contemporary urban folk art at The Barbican in July 2005 called 'Contemporary Popular Art from the UK') – 'If Pop Art is about liking things, as Andy Warhol said, then folk art is about loving things'. We could add that fine art is often about understanding things.

Some paintings, in particular, exist on the borderline between folk art and fine art, especially 19th century examples produced by amateur English artists. If such pieces have to be placed in one camp or the other the decision is likely to be made on commercial grounds rather than aesthetically. If folk art values are on the rise at a particular time it will probably win the day because there are many fewer folk art than fine art paintings in existence. The legions of amateur and professional Georgian and Victorian artists produced sufficient paintings to ensure that this imbalance will always apply.

With the possible exceptions of paintings and samplers, artists involved in the creation of amateur folk art pieces are rarely identifiable. They often followed the form and ornament of existing pieces such as love spoons or samplers rather than creating their own style. It is also very difficult to determine where many folk art pieces were made; some styles can be tied to particular parts of the country but only those that are signed or contain detailed dedications give us some chance to locate their origin. A simple inscription with the initials of the owner or maker do not automatically make a piece folk art, there has to be some artistic intent as well.

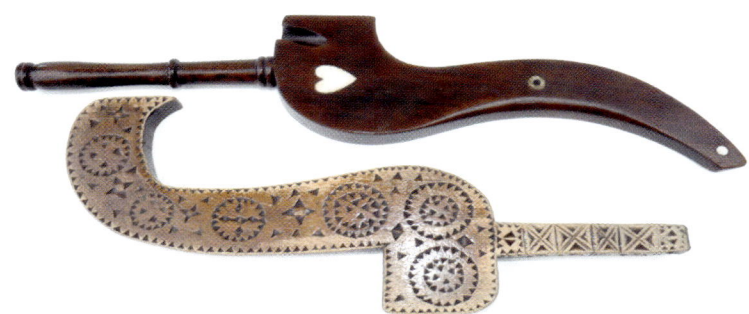

Two Goosewing Knitting Sheaths, 19th century. This style was predominately made in the Yorkshire Dales. 28 cms. C2-03.

Materials used in producing amateur folk art were generally those readily to-hand: wood, non-precious metals, wool, corn, stone, general scraps and so on. Techniques used were handed down through the generations and quality is usually less than professional. Looked at purely from the material employed, there are contradictions in accepted definitions of folk art. Glassware (which needs high temperatures not attainable in a normal fire) is usually excluded; pottery (which requires similar technical capabilities) is usually included. This anomaly seems to exist because the 'earthiness' of the material overcomes logical classification. Ironwork is often included because it was frequently hand-beaten into shape so it becomes a 'craft' industry. Brass, an alloy which is usually cast and therefore industrial, is usually excluded.

The older the piece, the harder it is to determine whether it is amateur or commercial folk art. The Lewis Chessmen date to c.1200 and were discovered in the early 19th century on the Isle of Lewis. Lewis was part of Scandinavia at this time so they could equally be considered Norwegian as British. They certainly have a folk art appeal but we cannot be sure whether they were part of a merchant's stock or a unique personal creation.

The Lewis Chessmen are in the British Museum, London. 8 cms.
C2-03.

In his book on primitive art (R2-07) Leonhard Adam suggests that the peasant art of today cannot be identified with the vision and vitality displayed in the artwork of early human civilisations. This is a valid point of view; his book looks at the very earliest art of prehistoric man on which everything following was to some extent based. Folk art, therefore, is derivative to a large extent.

Cow Creamer jug, Staffordshire, early 19th century. C3-01.

Chapter 3 - Commercial Folk Art

One objective of this book is to comment on the difference between commercial folk art and amateur folk art. There is a discernible distinction between professional, semi-professional, skilled amateur and enthusiastic amateur producers. For the purposes of this book the definition of commercial folk art is any object that was made in number to gain a profit. There are certainly objects that are not unique which would have been made for incidental profit but if they did not provide a livelihood for the creator they are not considered commercial folk art. It is unlikely, for example, that anyone made a living from producing corn dollies although they were certainly sold. On the other hand production of Staffordshire flatbacks would have kept the wolf from the door for many Potteries families in the 19th century.

Date of creation, if discernible, helps with a broad definition. While amateur folk art has been produced continually over the last 500 years its metamorphosis into a classifiable commercial commodity seems to have taken place from Elizabethan times onwards. In the late 16th century professional potteries such as Donyatt in Somerset were making decorated slipwares that we now qualify as folk art. In the 16th and 17th centuries makers of English oak furniture produced work that was closer to folk art than did their more refined contemporaries working elsewhere in Europe. Many professionals of the 18th and 19th centuries plied additional trades alongside their main employment. It was as common for blacksmiths to paint shop signs as it was for barbers to handle blood-letting. The many companies producing folk art throughout the nineteenth century had no inkling that their products would be labelled in this way in the twentieth and twenty-first centuries. Their focus was on producing colourful, decorative commercial goods at a low cost for which a market existed.

Carved and polychrome 16th century mystical beast. 11 cms. C3-02.

It is only now that we take an overall view of naïve 'country' items and bring them together under the folk art umbrella. This is also true of the output of potters producing delft and earthenware in the sixteenth, seventeenth and eighteenth centuries; the general population could not afford porcelain table-ware so the potters fulfilled this demand.

On the fringes of commercial folk art we can consider art potters and produc-ers of arts and crafts pieces around the turn of the 19th/20th centuries. In most cases their products were made for profit but they often sprang from the same vernacular sources as folk art. In their defence, the more unique pieces were made as much as vehicles of artistic expression as they were for commer-cial gain.

Sometimes it is the subject rather than the execution which places an object in the folk art camp. The toper Toby Philpot, subject of a million Toby Jugs, is usually a commercial folk art character even on the very rare occasions that he was reproduced in porcelain rather than earthenware.

Unusual wooden Toby Jug c.1850. 12.8 cms. C3-02.

Staffordshire Pearlware Toby Jug c. 1800. 25 cms. C3-02.

In terms of the material or process used to make them we can consider anything printed, fired, cast or made of glass as commercial folk art because of the facilities required to produce them. The quality of workmanship on these commercial pieces is variable. Pieces from a long run of moulded earthenware figures for example, may lack definition and detail of finish. Some of the more one-off pieces can be very skilfully produced.

It is not hard to find folk art for sale in the 21st century; however it is worth recognising that the vast majority of material which is given the label is commercial in origin. In many cases a market for amateur work prompted commercial production but to borrow a quotation 'if you call yourself a folk artist, you most likely are not one' (R3-01), and to find unique and artistically valuable contemporary work is rare . A good example of this more modern work is the customised 'Welsh Love Spoons' that proliferate on internet auction sites. Amateur 18th and 19th century love spoons are highly collected as often wonderful examples of early treen (see Chapter 9) but these much later copies are perfunctory in their attempts at originality.

Many 'Folk Art' trinkets are now churned out in countries with low labour costs to formulaic, cutesy designs. Early folk art has a much more artistically valuable history than these recent commercial expressions suggest. Retailers who create modern 'folk art' products miss the (aesthetic, not commercial) point - amateur folk art was rarely made to be sold. People who create 'folk art' based on instructional books and classes describing how it should be done are also misguided – any work made to an exact formula cannot really qualify as art. What these books actually do is further perpetuate the bland country style beloved of market traders, garden centres and a seemingly large proportion of the population.

Commercially-produced early 20th century treen sugar tongs for 'Mrs Lewis'. 16.2 cms. C3-02.

There is a great deal of souvenir ware in existence, especially from the late 19th and early 20th centuries. It is virtually all commercial and in almost every case not really folk art. It would be very difficult to qualify as folk art such items as Mauchline ware (objects made usually of sycamore bearing transfer images of seaside resorts, photographs and the like), Goss and Carlton crested china, shell ware seaside trinkets and Tunbridge Ware souvenirs. The same applies to the huge amount of commemorative ware that exists.

Mauchline ware sewing trinkets.
6.5 cms. C3-02.

Under commercial folk art we must consider deliberate fakes of earlier pieces. A great deal of material that purported to be 18th or 19th century was examined during research for this book; on examination most was at best copied or at worst, faked. Such copies, made to deceive, exist everywhere but are more prevalent in the USA than the UK because of the maturity and size of their market. In April 1988 a large exhibition of American folk art fakes next to the copied originals was assembled by the Museum of American Folk Art in New York. The accompanying catalogue (R3-02) identified how easy it is for copies (deliberate fakes or straightforward reproductions) to work their way into the market as 'genuine'. A maker of reproduction duck decoys saw an example of his recent work, originally sold for $16, at an antiques fair listed at $3,100 and had to work hard to convince the vendor to withdraw it. Once such a piece has been accepted as original by someone (and they have paid a 'full' price for it) it is very unlikely to be subsequently downgraded – if only because the owner has no wish to lose money on it. In this situation provenance becomes paramount. The only saving grace of the reproductions situation is that if the market is flooded with multiple copies of a particular item, dealers and collectors alike will back off very quickly. The advent of the internet has helped communicate such problems widely. Copies and fakes produced in ones and twos are still a problem; however they are often laboured and lack the spontaneity and genuine wear of original pieces.

Faking of British folk art goes back to the 19th century. Some of the earliest examples are 'Billy and Charleys', spurious cast lead copies of 14th century pilgrim's badges, figures and medals. They were made by two illiterate mud-larks, William Smith and Charles Eaton, in London in the 1850s. Realising that they could make more money from faking than from searching for original pieces on the Thames foreshore, they flooded the market with thousands of items their own manufacture, sold as originals found during excavations for the new docks at Shadwell.

19th century lead 'Billy and Charleys',
They are dated '1001' and '1000' respectively,
dates that would have correctly been written
'MI' and 'M' at that time.
10.7 cms. C3-02.

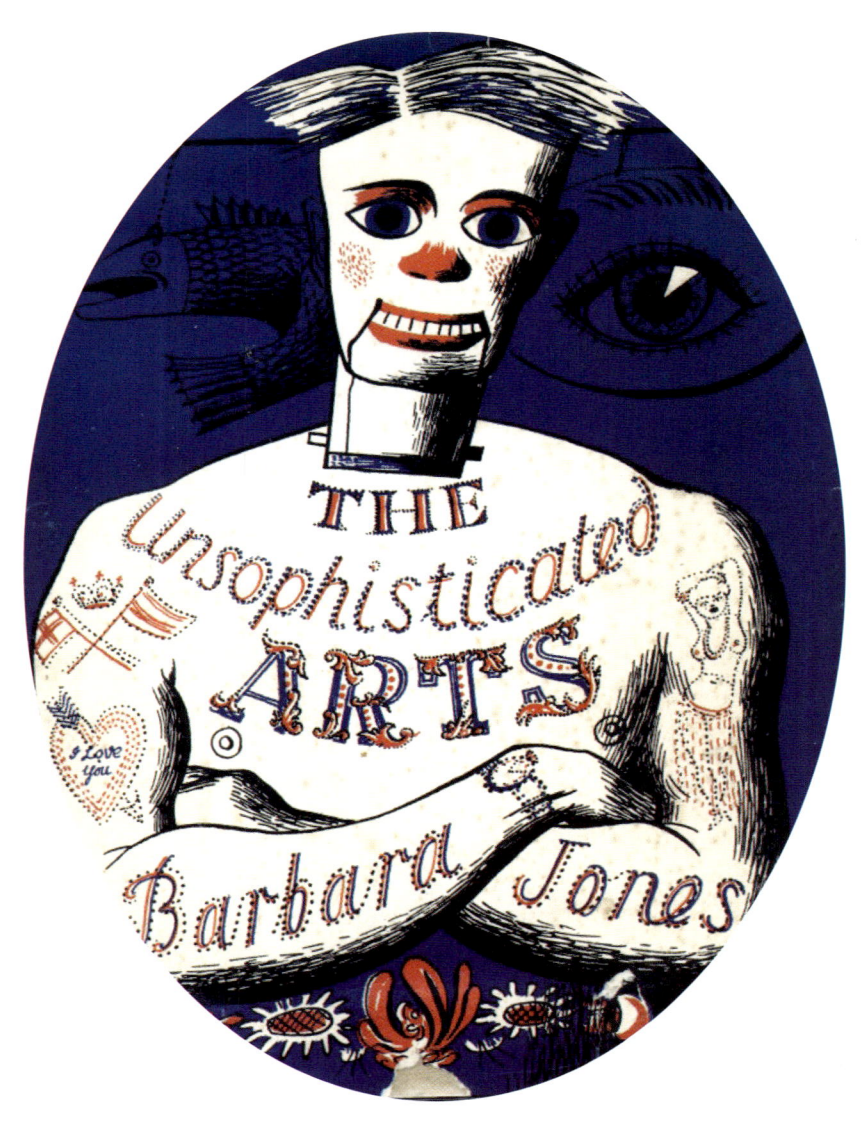

Cover illustration from *The Unsophisticated Arts*
by Barbara Jones. 1951

Chapter 4 - The History and Recognition of British Folk Art

Most British art of the middle ages was popular as opposed to fine. Fine art was based on classical rules from different cultures – Greek, Roman and the Italian Renaissance. Fine art was 'polite'. Folk art was 'rude'. It tended to be produced independently of these classical sources although their influence is inevitably seen. Folk art, for the most part, managed to completely ignore changes in contemporary design - Baroque, Rococo, the Romantic Movement, the Gothic Revival and so on were 'in the air' but had little impact. It also steered away from fads of fashion imported from the East - China, Japan, Egypt and elsewhere. In an early OED reference (R4-01) the author remarks how 'in Czech folk art can be detected the spirit of the Renaissance, Baroque, Rococo and Empire'. This is much less obvious with British folk art and it is all the better for this. The 'skill' of the creator of amateur folk art was in assimilating but not becoming overwhelmed by these outside influences. Resistance to the notion that 'wealthy people recognise fine art as being better … so it must be' enabled them to retain simplicity and kept them from the slippery slope of simply copying classical motifs.

By some definitions all art between classical Greek and Roman times and the Renaissance could be considered folk art but we can probably say that British folk art, as discussed in this book, started to be produced around the time that serfdom started to die out in the 1500s. When the influence of the English medieval craft guilds began to wane in the 16th century (they were actually abolished in 1835) their various techniques in working metal, wood and other materials became less of a mystery to the general population. Manuals (R4-02) were produced from the 17th century onwards encouraging amateurs (generally rich amateurs) to try their hand at oil painting, engraving, japanning and the like. The privileged backgrounds of those who had access to these books would have included exposure to the fine arts and although some of their efforts were quite naïve they don't really qualify as folk art. The production of these manuals continued into the 18th century.

Britain is a small country so fashions were relatively easily spread by the flow of trade from city to country. In the 18th and 19th centuries intellectual art was being formalised in England through organisations such as the Royal Academy and newly-established galleries. Their influence trickled slowly into folk art via the large network of country estates and mansions whose owners collected fine art and whose servants and workers became exposed to it.

Use of the word 'folk' conjures up gaily dressed peasants probably dancing round maypoles, singing, drinking and laughing. In reality the people who

produced amateur folk art were simple men and women for whom life was largely a slog. They were uneducated, illiterate and they left little in the way of contemporary records of the artwork they made. Of the 245 detailed farm and cottage inventories from 1635 – 1749 analysed in Steers' 1950 book (R4-03) very few (perhaps 5%) mention objects with any kind of decoration. These were the type of dwellings that we would expect to have contained some folk art objects so it is clear that little value was placed on them at that time.

Fairs such as St Bartholomew's Fair at Smithfield (which ended in 1850) involved much folk art, most of it decorative and displayed on rides and sideshows such as Punch and Judy rather than being offered for sale. It was there more for entertainment than for trade; the major purpose of these fairs was the sale of livestock and, occasionally, people. Some commercial folk art from these events does survive; this nutcracker would have been offered as a prize or sold for a few pence.

Early 19th century figural
fruitwood nutcracker
15 cms. C4-01.

In *Moby Dick* (1851) the American Hermann Melville acknowledged the power of primitive art as being equal to that of fine art. Britain was slow to even attempt this comparison and has never caught up with the value placed on folk art by the USA.

The Great Exhibition in 1851, conceived as a showcase for Britain's manufacturing industries, did not contain anything which we would recognise as folk art. It was similarly excluded from the Art Treasures Exhibition in Manchester in 1857. Much of the Victorian age was geared to mechanising production but throughout this time individuals, usually those away from towns and cities, were still expressing their individuality and documenting their lives in paintings and other one-off artefacts. There are isolated instances of the recognition of folk art values at this time; in 1866 the authors of *The History of Signboards* (R4-04) noted their regret at the disappearance of many significant inn signs which were a very vernacular form of public folk art.

Throughout the 19th century there were regular pageants and processions at which folk art was displayed on banners and signs. Icons such as Old Snap the Norfolk dragon and the Chester and Coventry Guild Giants would be paraded through the town often as part of a mayoral procession. Many trade associations displayed their insignia at the head of annual parades on large and often naïve banners. These public exhibitions of folk art gradually disappeared from view as entertainment moved into concert and music halls and, in the 20th century, into homes via radio, television and the internet.

Banner of the Amalgamated Society of Railway Servants for Scotland. This trade union existed from 1872 to 1892 when it merged with the English Amalgamated Society of Railway Servants, later to become part of the National Union of Railwaymen. C4-02.

The Industrial Revolution was to some degree responsible for the demise of folk art because the skills traditionally needed to construct utility items were no longer in demand. When a simple chair could be bought from a factory for a few shillings people were much less inclined to learn how to carve, whittle, turn and join wood. People started working in factories rather than at home, there was migration away from villages to towns and new technology and materials became available. Prior to the Industrial Revolution pastoral and sea-faring lives provided spells of free time that could be used to good effect as far as producing folk art was concerned. On farms there was a natural lull during the dark hours of winter and for sailors the time spent travelling to and from fishing grounds and when becalmed was available. It was during these times that many amateur artists took to decorating the tools of their trade or producing items for their families and sweethearts. When working in factories became more the norm the working day was regimentally defined, there was little 'down time' and time outside the long factory hours started to become 'leisure time'.

Folk art was generally excluded from the collecting boom that developed in Britain in the mid-to-late 19th century. Most collectors at that time (including museums) tended to look for antiquarian and classical objects from Greek, Roman, Egyptian and ancient British history. Even those that had an interest in 'bric-a-brac' or the 'lesser' arts looked for *refined* objects in silver, glass, china, textile and so on. Naiveté counted for little. It is likely that the odd piece of folk art passed through the hands of collectors such as Charlotte Schreiber or Joseph Mayer but they would only have been valued if they were of significant age or rarity. Early collectors were mostly literate middle- and upper-class and not particularly interested in the illiterate lower classes. In 1886 the famous Tippoo's Tiger was one of the few objects displayed at the V & A (then the South Kensington Museum) that we might recognise as folk art today. However it was only British in that it was made in the Empire - commissioned by the Sultan of Mysore to symbolise his opposition to British rule.

The introduction of compulsory education by the 1870 Education Act meant that people started to recognise a divide between work and leisure that had not previously existed. The wealth created by the Industrial Revolution meant that basic human survival needs were satisfied and free time that might have previously been used to craft works of folk art started to be filled with other leisure pursuits. Some folk art pursuits such as knitting and lace making did survive the Industrial Revolution but only on a much more limited, often craftwork basis.

In the late 19th century the aims of the Arts & Crafts movement helped to rejuvenate interest in folk art ideals. Socialism aside, William Morris's promotion of individualism in design and construction has much in common with folk art. Over a hundred Arts & Crafts Associations (such as the Cottage Arts Association) were formed in Britain in the late 19th/early 20th century. They encouraged people, particularly home-based women, to learn and hone their skills and to produce rural handicraft pieces. In 1911 over 5,000 pupils enrolled in courses run by the Home Arts and Industries Association, learning woodcarving, metalworking (brass, copper and silver), pottery, leatherworking and a range of textile work.

Academic interest in folklore came to the fore in the last few years of the 19th century when the Egyptologist Sir Flinders Petrie proposed a museum portraying the cultural history of the British Isles, in Surrey. Unfortunately his proposal came to nothing, as did a subsequent 1912 proposal by a group of eminent sponsors for the Crystal Palace to house a British Folk Museum. An early collection of peasant art from Europe and Scandinavia, included some British folk art objects, had been assembled in 1895 by the Reverend Gerald Davies. He donated it to the Peasant Arts Guild who, in 1925, passed it on to the Haslemere Educational Museum which still exists today.

It was around this time that interest in folk art started to take off in a big way in the United States. The first exhibition of American Folk Art took place in New York in 1924. It helped generate a collecting market which has always far outweighed the appetite in Britain for our own home-produced folk art. Interestingly there have been links between British and American folk art collecting through the years. The American Museum in Britain in Bath holds one of the largest and most important collections of American Folk Art outside the States and there have been exhibitions here – notably American Primitive Art at the Whitechapel Art Gallery in 1955.

In 1926 a Department of Folk Life was created as part of the National Museum of Wales but it was not until 1946 that a dedicated museum, the Welsh Folk Museum, was established in Wales. In 1928 the 'British National Committee on Folk Art' was established followed by a 'Folk Museum Committee' but lack of funding meant that their combined efforts came to nothing. A brief appraisal of folk art in a journal published in 1938 concluded that it was '… mostly of an uncultured nature'.

In his 1931 book *The Meaning of Art* Herbert Read dedicated several pages to what he called Peasant Art. He identified it as 'objects made by uncultured peoples in accordance with a native and indigenous tradition owing nothing to outside influences'. As a definition of folk art this stands up pretty well today.

Throughout the 1930s folk museums started to be formed; in 1936 a small folk museum opened on the island of Iona and in 1938 an open air museum at Gregneash, Isle of Man. Other museums with related holdings were opened pre-World War II, notably the Castle Museum in York. In 1951 the University of Reading established the Museum of English Rural Life, now situated in the centre of Reading. Its mission is to present a record of rural life relating to food, farming and the countryside and it is one of our more important resources.

The New Bodleian Library in Oxford holds the records of the Oxford Folk Art Society which existed from 1939 to 1959. This was a small group of people (membership varied between 4 and 58) who produced regular news sheets and achieved a little press coverage. Unfortunately they did not publish any papers of significance but they were one of the earliest British folk art interest groups.

British author Enid Marx (1902-1998) was an early enthusiast of folk art. She taught (including such luminaries as Peter Blake) at the Gravesend School of Art in the 1940s. At the end of the Second World War she commented that 'the "innocent eye" is disappearing' as she started to find fewer and fewer examples of popular art. She put this down to increased industrialism, increased urbanisation, changes in social habits and a general downturn in individuality.

The Festival of Britain in 1951 was aimed mainly at celebrating the nation's recovery after World War II so many of its exhibits were forward- rather than backward-looking. The mission of the Arts Council who mounted the Festival was 'to increase the accessibility of the fine arts to the public'. However as part of the Festival the Whitechapel Art Gallery presented an exhibition entitled 'Black Eyes and Lemonade' of 'British Popular and Traditional Art'. Its organisers, Barbara Jones (1912-1978) and Tom Ingram, struggled as we do today to find a workable definition of folk art; in the accompanying catalogue

Jones said 'we have not been able to find a satisfactorily brief and epigrammatic definition of Popular Art'. Her view was that older pieces tended to have been amateur folk art and newer pieces made by professionals. The exhibits (many of which were from Jones' own collection) varied between pieces contemporary with the exhibition and those one and two centuries old. Approximately seven hundred objects were put on show including many that we would still put in the folk art category today – ship figureheads, canal art, corn dollies, Staffordshire figures, sailor love tokens, animal portraits and Punch and Judy characters. They included an unusual Staffordshire jug which employs Napoleon's mouth as the spout and which appears as the frontispiece to this book, and a horse vertebra decorated as a clergyman very similar to the one illustrated in Chapter 10. There were also pieces that we certainly would not classify as folk art today such as Chelsea porcelain, cricket blazers and Goss china.

Barbara Jones was an artist and illustrator in her own right and she designed some of the murals for the Festival of Britain. She later proposed a 'Museum of the Popular Arts' which did not come to fruition.

1951 also saw the publication of two important books relating to folk art – *The Unsophisticated Arts* by Barbara Jones and *English Popular Art* by Margaret Lambert (1906-1995) and Enid Marx. Marx and Lambert were major champions of the genre from the 1950s to the early 1960s and as well as publishing two related books they organised an exhibition of Popular Art at the Museum of English Rural Life, Reading in 1958. In *The Unsophisticated Arts* Jones suggests the start of the Great War as the 'tombstone date' after which traditional popular arts declined sharply.

One of the first significant collections of folk art in Britain was started by John Judkyn in the early 1950s. Judkyn continued to collect until his death in 1963 and some of his collection was combined with that of American collector Dallas Pratt to create the American Museum in Bath.

A major collection of treen folk art, the Pinto Collection, was assembled by Edward Pinto (1901-1972) and made available to the public from his home near Northwood in 1955. Treen is now generally accepted to mean domestic wooden items, turned or carved, of size smaller than furniture. Pinto was interested in history, wood and craftsmanship and he pursued these three threads to assemble a very comprehensive collection of over 6,000 items. In 1969 the collection moved to the Birmingham Museum and Art Gallery where it is still displayed.

In 1959 an authoritative guide to the classification of folk culture, Folk Life : Collection & Classification, was published by The Museums Association (R4-05). Although its author commented that folk art was the initial impetus for the creation of folk museums he offered no definitive definition of the term nor any method of classifying it. In fact the guide barely mentions folk art.

During the 1970s, 1980s and 1990s more books were published on the topic. The bibliography lists many more but the most significant and in-depth works are :

Ayres J, *British Folk Art*
Ayres J, *English Naïve Art*
Brears P, *North Country Folk Art*
Young R, *Folk Art*

 As recently as 2000, a report commissioned by the Heritage Lottery Fund (R4-06) quoted Peter Brears as saying that it was 'extremely difficult for anyone to gain access to collections of English folk art, to such an extent that even its very existence has come to be in doubt'.

In September 2009 the Tate (funded by the Arts and Humanities Research Council) organised a series of seminars starting in April 2010 and aimed at identifying key research areas in the under-worked field of British Folk Art. The project was led by Dr Martin Myrone, a curator at Tate Britain, whose 2009 paper, Instituting English Folk Art, *Visual Culture in Britain*, is a detailed academic study of folk art in Britain. The results of these seminars were not available when this book went to print. A related event, 'The Folk Art Debate' at Compton Verney in June 2011, advertised as an exploration of historical and contemporary perspectives of folk art was unfortunately cancelled due to lack of interest (six tickets were sold).

The only other initiative that the author is aware of is the Museum of British Folklore project led by Simon Costin. Once funding is in place this is intended to be a permanent museum covering a wide range of folklore objects and practices.

Pottery wall plaque, probably Sunderland, c. 1880, in
the form of a framed picture with religious motto.
The display of religious texts such as this in private
houses was commonplace during Victorian times and
into the 20th century. The plaques were produced in
large numbers and multiple formats – circular, square
and rectangular with various mottoes and borders.
Many had the all-seeing eye of God at the top.
21.4 cms. C5-02.

Chapter 5 - Folk Art Design Motifs

Inspiration for folk art designs often came from nature – flowers, plants and animals were physically nearby and were therefore used as simple decoration on country objects, particularly for the amateur. As well as straightforward physical representations, emotional subjects abound. Love tokens for a sweetheart or mother include hearts and various rebus devices such as forget-me-nots together with dedications of affection.

Designs were sometimes influenced by the material in use. Textiles with a square or rectangular warp and weft lend themselves more easily to patterns based on regular angles (90 degrees, 45 degrees and so on). Use of a potter's wheel discourages regular angles and encourages wavy patterns. Straightforward geometry also played a major part. Basic shapes – squares, triangles, circles and divisions thereof – were used singly and in combination to build up complex overall designs.

British folk art is usually secular, relating to home, nature and family rather than to religious beliefs. Biblical references were only occasionally included. This dearth of religious imagery is probably because of Britain's non-conformist and protestant background; in strongly catholic countries such as France and Germany there is a firm tradition of carved saints, crucifixes and religious symbols.

Children's folk art was often educational, containing scripts, parables and practising the alphabet - for example in samplers and horn books.

The most-reproduced form in British folk art is that of man himself, especially human facial images. The pronounced lentoid eyes on this nutcracker suggest a link to Celtic sources.

Early 17th century nutcracker.
20.2 cms. C5-01.

Subjects for human, animal and zoomorphic representations came from folk-lore (the King Charles Tree, the Wicker Man, the Green Man) from myth (the Rottingdean Imp, Cornish Piskies), and legend (Robin Hood). Characters from popular entertainment were also used. 'Punch and Judy' was established in England in the late 17th century from an ancestry in the Italian Commedia dell'Arte; Samuel Pepys records seeing Mr Punch in Covent Garden in his Diaries. As time went by the story was anglicised with the addition of characters such as Jack Tar, Jack Ketch, Toby the Dog and the Policeman. These characters help to demonstrate something of a more sinister side of folk art; there is an undercurrent of cruelty and fear in the representation (and performance) of Punch and Judy and similar objects such as ventriloquists dummies.

Rather spooky early 20th century
fairground marionette made of
wood, wire and papier mache.
58 cms. C5-01.

This undercurrent of cruelty was witnessed
in more serious rituals involving amateur
folk art effigies such as the display and burning of Guy Fawkes on the 5th November
(still to this day), the procession and burning
of 'Bartle' in West Witton, Wensleydale in
late August and even the Hitler effigies that
were defiled by crowds in Leeds on V.E. Day.
Frightening scarecrows have been made and
displayed since at least the mid-16th century
and some scarecrow festivals are still held
today.

The fact that many folk art objects were
retained, and often treasured, in domestic environments at least gives us the
chance to study and comment on their
design. It is harder to trace the development of more ephemeral folk art such
as the 'sanding' of streets in Knutsford,
Cheshire which involves the creation,
for one day, of patterns and mottoes on
the ground. Oral transmission of ideas
and stories was important in both permanent and non-permanent folk art.

'Sanding the Street' in Knutsford on
Royal May Day 1920

Some British folk art has been influenced by the influx of peoples from main-land Europe. One example is the Romany people who originated in Eastern Europe and whose direct influence can be seen in British Gipsy caravans, in fairground rides and in floral canal boat decoration. This is a rich design source and their love of baroque gilded décor with elaborate scripted lettering proliferated in the late 19th and early 20th centuries in many institutions and situations now no longer with us – ice-cream carts, music halls, tobacconist shops, tiled butcher shops, tiled dairies and elaborate city pubs.

Folk art designs can be surprisingly similar throughout the world, particularly where the countries have a shared ancestry. It would be difficult indeed to dif-ferentiate between many pieces of Breton and English design.

Trying to pre-date the influences already described is difficult. Perhaps the earliest influence identifiable is that of the Celts. These were a people who oc-cupied much of central Europe from the 6th century BC until their existence was threatened by the advancing Roman armies in the 2nd century BC. The British Isles became one of the last outposts of Celtic culture and their influ-ence is recognisable right up to the 6th century AD – both before and after the Roman period. Britain's four-century dominance by the Romans added their influence to Celtic art but once they had left these shores the early La Tene (R5-01) design traditions developed into an even more sophisticated set of motifs.

Surviving Celtic art consists largely of metalware and stone sculpture. Met-alware was produced to adorn swords and chariots, for use as tableware and as personal jewellery. Their designs were either for the general adornment of personal items or were a reflection of religious and ritual beliefs. Although they included some naturalistic human and animal representations it is the wide range of geometric designs that seem to have had a lasting influence. These designs were precision-drawn using patterns, compasses and painstak-ing draughtsmanship.

Much of the early metalware treasure in our museums was not discovered until the 19th and 20th centuries so they would have had limited impact on creators of folk art in the intervening period. However Celtic art would have been visible to later ages solely through their stone sculptures which prolifer-

ate (as gravestones, crosses and standing stones) from the 7th century onwards. They are found throughout the British Isles but particularly in Ireland
(as high crosses), Scotland and the Isle of Man where Celtic art was most
developed.

 These pieces of metalware were made to such an advanced degree of sophistication that they fall outside any definition of folk art. Anglo-Saxon art from
the Dark Ages was particularly highly developed. For a period starting in the
4th century and ending with the arrival of the Normans in the 11th century
these visitors from the Netherlands, Northern Germany and Denmark created
many precious pieces of jewellery.

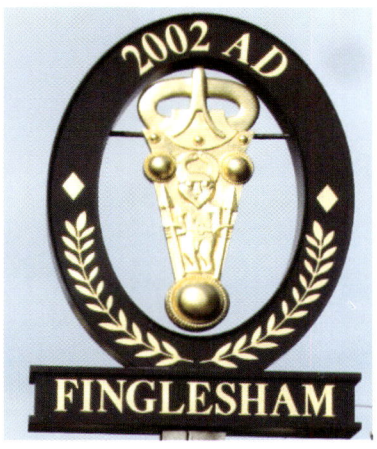

An Anglo-Saxon belt buckle depicting
the god Odin was discovered in the
Kent village of Finglesham in 1964 and
is now featured on their village sign.

Anglo-Saxon design influence survives in combinations of writhing serpents
and snakes, dogs, boars, birds (especially ravens) and complex interwoven
patterns. A set of simple basic motifs developed into more complex Celtic
knotwork forms which can be seen throughout British folk art :

The original development of Celtic art ceased around the time of the Norman Conquest in 1170 but it has been consistently revived since. The 16th century saw instances of the Celtic interlock shape in Scottish applied art; 17th century powder horns bore these same motifs as did many 19th century arts

and crafts pieces. Circular apotropaic symbols intended to prevent evil forces from coming down the chimney are sometimes found in 17th and 18th century buildings. Their form often resembles the basic Celtic divided circle.

9th century celtic Irish figure (reproduction), reputedly taken from Ireland by Viking raiders.
11.4 cms. C5-01.

Humour is often present in folk art; these 'Biting Beasts' from the Celtic Book of Durrow (7th century AD) are reminiscent in form and humorous attitude to misericords (wooden church carvings) of the 15th century and to later 18th and 19th century interpretations.

It is impossible to assemble a definitive list of all of the design motifs found in British folk art – what a dull art form it would be if we could predict it exactly. There are however a set of broad categories from which the majority of designs are drawn :

Calligraphy	- Monograms, inscriptions and messages
Family and political events	- Particularly birth, marriage and death
Geometric shapes	- From simple cross-hatching to magic knots and compass-drawn roundels
Heraldry	- Crowns, lions and unicorns
Literary works	- Paradise Lost, Pilgrims Progress etc.
Love and Good Fortune	- Hearts, arrows, keys
Man	- Human images, particularly heads and faces
Mythology	- Fabled creatures such as the Green Man, King Arthur
Nature	- Images of plants, animals and birds
Religion	- Biblical images such as Adam and Eve, The Cross
Trades	- Images of tools or trade symbols for black smiths, wheelwrights etc.

Modern copy of a jug excavated in London and dating
to the mid-14th century. 21 cms. C6-06.

Chapter 6 - Ceramics and Glass

Because of its origins and the technicality of its production we can generally exclude porcelain from the folk art ceramics genre. The decoration and form of early English porcelain (copying Chinese and German originals) places it some distance from folk art. The temperatures and technical know-how needed to fire pottery were way beyond the capabilities of amateurs so practically all British folk art ceramics can be considered commercial folk art.

British folk art ceramics date back to medieval times. Simple earthenware jugs were made in various parts of the country, especially it seems in London, from the 13th century onwards. Many were plain but some featured human masks not unlike later Toby jugs; some were humorous puzzle jugs which required the pourer to know exactly where to place his fingers to avoid a soaking.

Most country pottery was simply made and left undecorated. It is usually pieces that were made for special occasions (such as harvest time) or to mark special events (marriages and christenings) that are now valued folk art. These vessels were likely to have been produced by the village potter who was often a farmer or blacksmith too. Pottery was either thrown on a wheel, slab-built from sheets of clay or (for flatware) pressed into a mould. It was then fired in a kiln at between 1000 and 1100 degrees Celsius.

The simplest form of decorated pottery has inscribed decoration made directly into the clay which is then fired without further process. The development of slipware pottery c.1600 took this a step further. It was glazed with a lead glaze and decorated using different colour clays in creamy slip (that is, watered-down clay) form. Slip was dipped and trailed onto the body and further enhanced by incised *sgraffito* decoration. The most celebrated early producers of these wares were Staffordshire potters such as Thomas, James and Ralph Toft, Ralph Simpson and William Talor (sic) who were working in Staffordshire in the later 17th century.

Thomas Toft charger, North Staffordshire, 1670-1690. It is inscribed 'Smoke / your / Nose' .47 cms. C6-01.

Although practical tableware in form, much of this early slipware was intended for display only, it is unlikely that many meals were taken from Toft family chargers.

Slipware armorial dish, probably Barnstaple North Devon, dated 1748. 47.3 cms. C6-02.

Slipware Lion dish, possibly North Staffordshire, early to mid 18th century. 35 cms. C6-01.

The availability of local deposits of suitable clay often lead to a small local industry. In North Devon the Fremington clay area near Barnstaple supported several potting families including the Fishleys - George, Edmund, Robert and Edwin. The most highly prized of these Devon pieces now are what we now know as harvest jugs, large documentary pieces with multiple images and messages which were also made in Wales and in Donyatt in Somerset.

A further view of the 1741 harvest jug pictured at the start of Chapter One. C1-02.

Other centres producing folk art slipware pieces included Wrotham in Kent and Ewenny in Wales. Many regions had their own specialities such as Sussex 'Pig' drinking vessels and harvest barrels and stoneware Nottingham bear jugs. Halifax produced wedding cradles and chest-of-drawer shaped moneyboxes. Multi-handled drinking mugs known as tygs originated in Wrotham.

Delightfully simple little slipware cup, early 18th century, probably North Staffordshire. 5.7 cms. C6-01.

Puzzle Jug from Donyatt, Somerset, dated 1798. The inscription reads 'When thes you / W H / drink of me / See remember mee 1798 hand be merry B'. 16 cms. C6-01.

North Staffordshire posset pot, dated 1692. It has combed decoration on the lower body and a jewelled inscription including the makers name 'GEORGE TAYLOR'. The 'feathered' design on the lower body is typical.
11.4 cms. C6-01.

'Ozzie Owl' copy by West Yorkshire potter John Hudson, 20th century.
21.5 cms. C6-06.

The most publicized piece of Staffordshire slipware of recent years is the 'Ozzie Owl' jug which came to light on the BBC Antiques Roadshow in 1990. It was made in c.1680 in lead-glazed earthenware and has combed and trailed slip decoration representing the bird's feathers. At the time of discovery it was considered to be folk art pottery of the rarest kind. In fact after the Antiques Roadshow programme went to air, ten further examples quickly came to light, so it was recognised as much more a commercial product than a one-off piece of folk art modelling. Since this discovery several British potters have started producing commercial copies, some true to the original (such as the one illustrated) and some less so.

Slipware dish with stag, dated 1736 and made in the Midlands or North Staffordshire. The initials 'S M' would normally be attributed to the maker Samuel Malkin but this dish is very different to other Malkin wares. 34.9 cms. C6-01.

Slipware dish with imaginary bird, dated 1772, Midlands. 35.2 cms. C6-01.

A fine example of a contemporary slipware charger made by potter Clive Hickinbottom. 32 cms. C6-06.

Slipware moneybox with modelled chickens
and trailed spots c.1830, probably from
Burton in Lonsdale. 16.5 cms. C6-01.

English delftware, like slipware, has a pottery body but it was covered with
a white tin-glaze. It was made in the 17th and 18th centuries in imitation of
oriental porcelain, mainly in an attempt to provide an affordable alternative to
these high cost imports. As a consequence of this much delft carried images
copied directly from imported Chinese porcelain and is not really considered
folk art. However there are many wonderful surviving folk art pieces of delft,
perhaps the most famous of which are the 'blue-dash' chargers, named after
their distinctive borders and bearing very spontaneous portraits of royalty,
Adam and Eve and imaginary birds. As well as chargers, posset pots, barbers
bowls, fuddling cups, puzzle jugs, punch bowls, wine bottles and plates were
made.

London delftware Adam and Eve 'blue-dash' charger, c.1670. 32.8 cms. C6-03.

The main centres for British delft production were London, Liverpool and Bristol; surprisingly Staffordshire does not seem to have tended to this market. These British products bear direct comparison with the faience and maiolica earthenware from continental Europe at this time –Rouen, Alsace and Quimper. British delft was superseded by the introduction of cheaper and more robust Staffordshire creamware towards the end of the 18th century.

Bristol delft 'Farmyard' plate c. 1720-30. The 'trees' have been added using sponged manganese. 22.2 cms. C6-03.

Lambeth delft 'fox' dish, c.1740.
29.3 cms. C6-02.

Delftware plate c. 1740. 22.6 cms.
C6-03.

Delftware puzzle jug, Bristol or London, c. 1760. By covering two of the three spouts and a hidden hole on the handle the contents could be poured or sucked from the third spout via the hollow handle. 19 cms. C6-03.

Here Gentlemen come t
I'll hold a wager if yo
That you don't drink thi
Without you spill or l

In time the original utility-only purpose of folk art pottery was added to by pieces that were made for purely decorative purposes such as this 'Pew Group' based on a mid-18th century Staffordshire original. The name pew group is misleading, these were secular objects and the 'pew' was usually a kitchen settle.
17.5 cms. C6-06.

Pottery of all types was usually hand-made (either thrown or press-moulded) in the 17th, 18th and early 19th centuries but by the mid-19th century volume slip-casting had taken over. Being handmade contributes greatly to the folk art qualities of the earlier pieces. There is no substitute for the connection made with the past by seeing a 200-year old potter's fingerprint preserved in the clay. Much pottery shared decorative subject matter: royal events and insignia, biblical stories, humorous rhymes, floral and bird designs, animals and personal dedications.

The ubiquitous Toby Jug was first produced in Staffordshire in the late 18th century by either Ralph Wood of Burslem, John Astbury of Shelton or Thomas Whieldon of Frenton. As well as confusion over the maker there are several differing theories as to their origins. They could have been based on a print of a well-known Yorkshire toper, Toby Fillpott, or maybe on Uncle Toby from *Tristram Shandy* by Laurence Sterne. Perhaps there was a link to the names Low Toby (an 18th century footpad or mugger) or High Toby (a highwayman). In any event they were a firmly commercial product and are probably unique in that they have been produced up to the current day in one form or another. Their original purpose was to dispense ale but they were difficult to keep hygienically clean so they quickly became purely decorative. Many examples survive but rarely with their cover which was modelled as the top of Toby's hat.

Staffordshire Pearlware
Toby jug c. 1800.
C6-09.

Prattware is a generic term for a class of cream and pearlware made in the late 18th and early 19th century with bright underglaze coloured decoration. A company called Messrs F & R Pratt was one of the first manufacturers but there were perhaps ten or fifteen other suppliers. What takes some Prattware into the folk art category is the bright and naïve designs that were used. This is not so true of many other ceramic products of the 19th century such as English Majolica (often very colourful but not really naïve), Doulton wares (handsome but often formal) and the myriad of 'refined' china and porcelain wares by Bow, Chelsea, Derby et al. Relief decorated jugs with scenes such as 'The Sailors Return and Farewell' and 'Smokers and Drinkers' were the most common Prattware products but mugs, busts, cow creamers and novelty items were also made.

Coiled Prattware novelty pipe, early 19th century, Staffordshire or Yorkshire. 22.5 cms. C6-03.

In the late 18th and early 19th century there was a vogue for popular news subjects of the day to be portrayed on cheap pottery products. Decoration was both hand-painted and transfer-printed and many survive. Political events such as the repeal of the Corn Laws were celebrated with 'God Speed the Plough' slogans, engineering triumphs such as the Ironbridge in Shropshire and early railway developments such as The Rocket often resulted in commemorative plates and jugs. Sunderland lustre jugs and plaques were made with portrayals of ships and sometimes admonitory religious texts such as 'Thou God See'st Me'.

Sunderland lustreware jug c. 1835.
The Sunderland potteries were particularly
celebrated for this type of lustreware, made
by adding thin films of various metals to the
surface. This is a marriage piece celebrating
the marriage of Robert and Elizabeth Foster.
The hand painted decoration includes a 'crest'
of woodworkers tools and a religious motto.
23 cms. C6-05.

In Staffordshire many folky figure groups were made
of subjects which included animals, murderers, preachers, Queen Victoria, Grace Darling, Wellington,
Gladstone, the death of Nelson and, oddly, Potash
Farm (where a gruesome murder took place).
Many a home was cheered by the presence of
a 'flat-back' on the mantelpiece. None of these
were attempts at producing works of 'Art',
they were objects that were quick to produce,

Staffordshire Flatback figurine of a
boy seated in an arbour, c.1860. 10
cms. C6-06.

colourful, cheap, and representative of something in the contemporary public consciousness. Commercial considerations sometimes meant that the same mould was used for completely different subjects via the judicious application of different colours to create a new face and new clothes. Extras such as leafy 'bocage' and black printed quotations on the base sometimes added a feel of quality.

A pearlware bull-baiting group, c. 1810. 30 cms. C6-02.

During the 19th century a large amount of 'treacle glazed' pottery was produced. It had a thick opaque appearance and was intended as decorative and useful ware for the lower- and middle-class consumer. Most of it is anonymous and of middling quality but it has a very attractive naïve quality.

Treacle glazed chest-of-drawers moneybox dated '1898'. 13.5 cms. C6-06.

Late 19th century treacle glazed pottery bird whistle. 9.5cms . C6-06.

A further pottery variation called Spongeware was made in Staffordshire, Wales and Scotland from c.1800, again to satisfy the lower end of the domestic market. Decoration was handled both at the factory and via home piecework where shaped sponges were used to impress and spatter simple motifs and mottled finishes on earthenware pots, plates, jugs and novelty moneyboxes.

Measham ware was made in the final quarter of the 19th century and is closely associated with life on canal narrow boats. Barge owners would commission pieces annotated with their own messages using printer's type which was pressed into the damp clay. The decorative flowers, birds and so on were made separately and 'sprigged' onto the body. Huge teapots up to sixteen inches (40 centimetres) high were made with a subsidiary small teapot acting

Bargeware Teapot made by a potter called Mason c. 1890. Brown-glazed pottery with the inscription 'A Present from mother to C.O.Lewsbury 1891'. 16 cms. C6-04.

Unusual Bargeware Teapot decorated with marbled slip. Plaque impressed 'MR M BREARLEY HUCKNALL TORKARD'. c.1900. 31.5 cms. C6-07.

The production of folk art pottery did not cease at the end of the 19th century but it did slow significantly. Some of the work of British art potters such as Bernard Leach and Michael Cardew referred back to country pots from earlier centuries but the influence of Japan moved most of it into a different sphere. It does require a small stretch of the imagination but some of the more naïve output of factories such as Poole Potteries, Susie Cooper, Clarice Cliff and Troika could be classed as folk art.

Slip decorated bowl by Michael
Cardew at Winchcombe Pottery,
Gloucestershire, c.1937. 36 cms.
C6-01.

Chapter 6 Cont'd - Glass

Like ceramics, glassware was not a medium available to most individuals for the production of amateur folk art. The main products of glassworks in the late 18th and early 19th centuries were window glass and everyday drinking vessels. Some early wine and ale glasses carried inscriptions naïve enough to qualify them as folk art but most decoration was of a more refined nature.

Pieces of leftover glass would be used to make small one-off items such as witches balls, walking canes, rolling pins and 'friggers' – small decorative nick-nacks also known as 'foreigners', end-of-days' or 'walk-outs'. Several small workshops were established in London specifically to make these kind of items from recycled bottles.

Glass rolling pins were sometimes decorated naïvely with messages such as 'A Present from Hartlepool' and were sold to sailors as gifts for their wives and sweethearts. Rolling pins with corked ends are thought to have been used to smuggle scent into Britain from abroad. Other glass rolling pins were decorated using the decalcomania technique in a similar way to the wooden example pictured in Chapter 10. All of these pieces are commercial folk art.

Painted Bristol blue glass rolling pin depicting a sailing ship called 'Providence'. It is inscribed 'Redbridge 1855' and 'John Parker Land-lord of the Ship Tap'. There is a Redbridge near Southampton on the South Coast and there is still a Ship Inn in the vicinity.
31.5 cms. C6-06.

North East glass rolling pin nail-engraved with images of the Wear
Bridge, a sailing ship, a steamship, a steam engine and the name
'Susana Brown Ray'. c.1845. 37 cms. C6-06.

Very large Bristol blue glass rolling pin c.1870. It would possibly have been
filled with tea and corked at the end. Images include a sailing ship and various mottoes such as 'COME BOX THE COMPASS' and 'LOVE AND BE
HAPPY'. 75 cms. C6-06.

'Token of Love' enamelled patch box c.
1800, probably made in Bilston, West
Midlands.
Patches were originally applied to the
face to disguise facial blemishes such as
smallpox scars. By this time they had become fashion items, worn to emphasise
the whiteness of the skin. It has a little
mirror for application in the lid.
3.7 cms. C6-06.

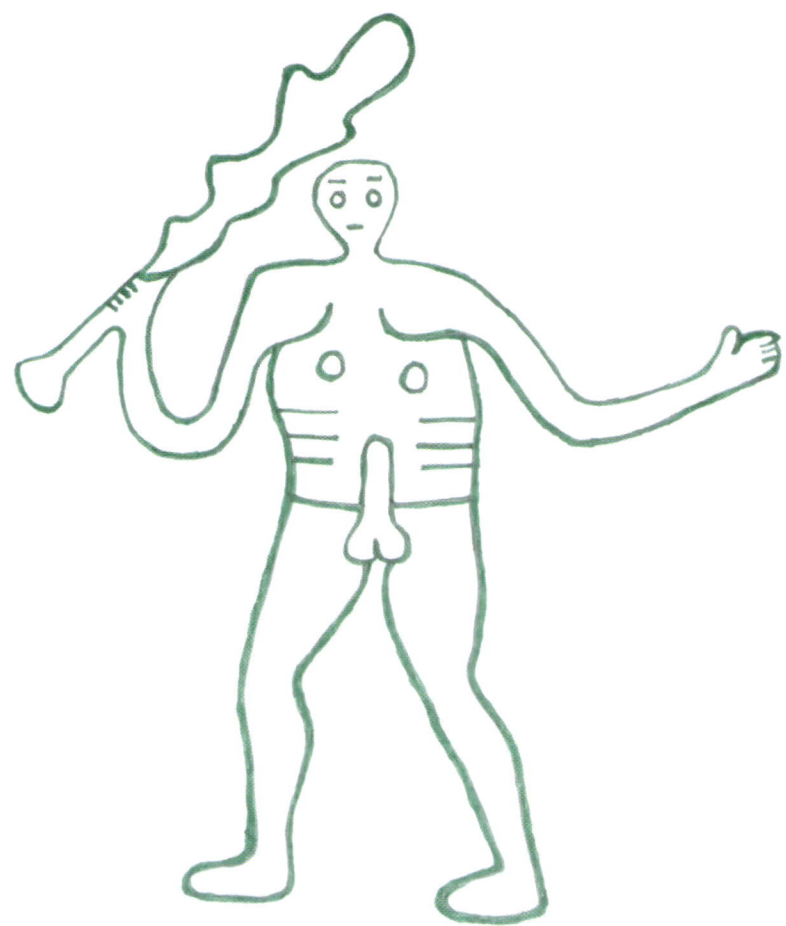

The Cerne Abbas Giant in Dorset

Chapter 7 - Paintings, Signs and Sculptures

British primitive and folk art painting did not start to be seriously appreciated until well into the 20th century. An article written by Margaret Lambert and Enid Marx in 1950 (R7-01), prompted by the already well-established market for American naïve works, was trumpeted as the first report on the subject. Interestingly the adjective naïve is applied much more frequently to paintings than it is to other folk art objects. It is perfectly valid in both cases so perhaps this is just a reflection of the dominance of paintings (over other objects) in the marketplace.

Of course naïve British folk art images go back a very long way; there are more than thirty major figures cut out of the grass and chalk on Britain's hillsides which were created as religious symbols, way markers and to simply decorate the landscape. The best-known examples are the Long Man of Wilmington, the possibly pre-Christian Cerne Abbas Giant and the White Horse at Uffington. Purists might argue that they are not paintings but they are some of the earliest examples of British folk art and warrant inclusion here.

Unlike elsewhere in Europe, the exterior walls of British buildings were not habitually decorated with paintings. Decorative exterior plasterwork (pargeting) was sometimes used, particularly in London, Suffolk and East Anglia. Interior wall paintings, the early English equivalent of frescoes, are now quite rare survivors. Some early (12th century and before) wall paintings do survive in English churches. Their use in domestic settings is rarer. Because they were painted directly onto absorbent plaster, making corrections difficult, they often have a charming spontaneity similar to that of early biscuit-painted delftware.

From Tudor times the travelling professional portrait painter, or limner, was a familiar figure, making his rounds of country fairs and houses. The term limner was originally applied to artists producing watercolours but is now used generally for travelling artists. In *The Vicar of Wakefield* (1766) by Oliver Goldsmith such a limner paints a portrait of the whole Primrose family. By far the major proportion of folk art paintings that we see today were made on this professional basis. As well as providing a straightforward record of family and possessions many were commissioned to glorify the subject, be it human or animal. Pictures of prize cattle, horses, sheep and pigs were normally commercially-produced.

The Teeswater Ox, c.1785, Unknown
C7-02.
This is an early painting of a prize farm animal, a Teeswater Shorthorn. It would have been commissioned by its owner to show his contemporaries what fine breeding animals he had produced. The animal is of normal, that is not highly modified, proportions. Later pictures were often of intensively bred stock with proportions not normally seen in nature.

Comet, 1811, Thomas Weaver
C7-02.
Comet was a prize light roan shorthorn bull that was sold in 1810 for 1,000 guineas – a huge sum at that time. He was calved in 1804 and died in 1815.

Naïve domestic family portraits developed when the middle classes started to attain wealth which they were keen to exhibit on their walls. Academic portraiture was always the province of the upper classes.

South View of Fen End Farm.
watercolour and ink on paper,
dated 20th Aug 1790.
Initialled M.S.L., 41.5 cms.
C7-01

The Indefatigable, post-1796, Unknown. C7-17.
This wonderfully detailed oil painting depicting the British ship Indefatigable was probably produced by a sailor. She is engaging with a French warship in 1796 and is surrounded by images of Britannia, Fame and Hope. The legend in the oval top right reads: His Majesty's ship Indefatigable of 40 guns. Sir Edw. Pellow engages and takes La Verginia a French Frigate of 44 guns on the 22nd April 1796 off the coast of France Neptune and Amphitrite god and goddess of the Seas Riding Triumphant. In fact the British vessel surrendered after a long chase.

The Sunbeam, a woolwork and silk picture dating from c.1880. Sunbeam, a 323-ton three-masted schooner, was built in 1874 and scrapped in 1929. This picture was made by a Royal Artillery gunner. C7-17.

Technical developments aided the development of true amateur folk art painters. Watercolour paints in 'cake' form were introduced by Reeves Brothers in London in the 1780s and from the 1840s oil paint in metal tubes (invented by John Rand in the United States) became available. This meant that there was no longer any need for potential artists to grind and mix their own pigments as professional artists always had.

In folk art painting generally, each brushstroke counts for something, there is little attempt at creating the impression of, say, the apples on a tree, they are explicitly painted one by one. They have defined outlines and are placed carefully in positions that are more likely to be representative of nature rather than reproducing nature. In practice, some would be obscured by others and by foliage and branches but the typical folk art interpretation is to draw each one, often evenly spaced over the treetop. Every brushstroke relates directly to something that physically exists, there is no use of complex techniques to suggest an object. Amateurs often tended to include domestic pets and sometimes an element of storytelling in their pictures.

There is usually little attempt at correctly representing the relative size of objects in the foreground and background. Children often appear bigger than houses. As painting gets more sophisticated this one-to-one relationship of object and image gets less pronounced. Amateur paintings of family and friends usually exhibit some attempt at representing the particular personality of the person or animal. It is a truism that 'paintings with teeth' are often folk art paintings; few professional fine art portraits included people showing their teeth (which was considered impolite in Victorian society) whereas many folk art paintings did.

Returning from a Bad Market, Butter Only One and Nine, oil on canvas, c. 1815.
It seems that the farmer on the right is not happy with the prices he has realised at market (I hate to see People Grinning !). The woman, on the other hand, seems very content with her purchases. C7-17

Admiral Lord Exmouth, ink watercolour and gouache on paper, c. 1815.
Lord Exmouth, Edward Pellow (1757-1833), joined the navy at the age of 13 and saw action in the War of American Independence. He later became Vice-Admiral and Viscount, captaining The Indefatigable (ibid.). The unsuccessful perspective of the stairs behind the figure in this painting is typical of folk art. The furniture in the foreground is tiny by comparison with the figure and the deer are individually plonked into the field rather than being naturalistically grouped. The attempt at foreshortening his shoes is also rather odd. C7-17

It is likely that early professional sign painters developed the fashion for promotional livestock paintings that lasted from c.1780 until they were replaced by photography c.1900. As time went on these painters started to appear in trade directories listed as 'decorative and pictorial artist'. There are few purely landscape folk art paintings, landscape is normally used as a background for a portrait, animal or story picture.

Three Sober Preachers, c.1860, Unknown.
The texts hanging on the wall are at odds with the
fact that the figures are preachers.
The text in the frames on the wall read : I Say
Brothers, We Are three Clever Fellows to Preach
Against Tippling / Tippling Do you say, I call this
Down Right, Hard Drinking / You may say what
you Please Gentlemen but I think Wine makes Our
Hearts Merry. C7-18

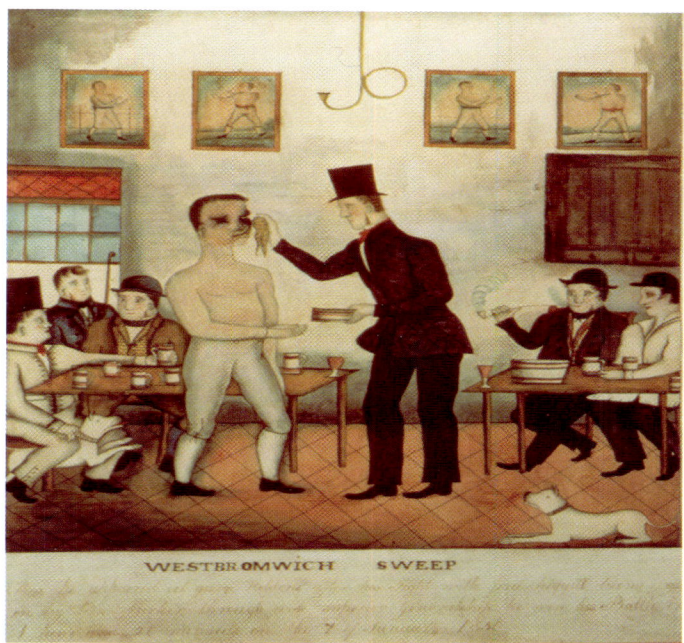

West Bromwich Sweep, water-colour, c.1850, depicting the scene after a fight lasting one hour and twenty minutes. Jem Parker, mentioned in the caption, was the Sweep's manager. C7-18

Still Life, signed 'G J Beech 1891'. This is a good example of the kind of still life painting produced over and over again by late 19th century amateurs. The table is set for a good basic meal of bread, cheese and beer. The Joule brewery is still in existence today. 38 cms. C7-04.

Old Man and Donkey, 1833, George Smart (1775-1846) C7-18

George Smart was a tailor from Frant, near Tunbridge Wells. He added scraps of material to underlying engravings that he also coloured using watercolour. This is a recognisable location in Frant; the figure is Old Bright, the postman. Smarts' work was collected by Queen Victoria's uncle, the Duke of Sussex.

As well as conventional watercolour (the favoured amateur medium) and oil paintings, mixed media pictures are worthy of note. They usually had a foundation in a painted image that was enhanced by the addition of other materials and were often amateur works. Anything to-hand was used – shells, hair, sand, fabric, straw, feathers and rope all featured.

Population Explosion, 1965, Elizabeth Allen (1883-1978) 47.6 cms. C7-17

Patchwork on canvas picture that depicts a contemporary story about a woman who gave birth to seven stillborn babies after taking a fertility drug. The picture employs felt, cotton, bias binding, nylon and broderie anglaise. Elizabeth Allen, a tailor's daughter, continued the tradition of folk art collage in the 20th century. Her pictures, often depicting stories from current affairs, were made of any scraps of material that were to-hand.

Professionally-produced paper or card silhouettes ('shades' or 'poor man's miniatures') were very popular prior to the invention of photography. They were inexpensive commercial folk art and could be cut within one or two minutes. Amateur silhouettes were also made but they usually fail to reproduce a recognisable image of an individual.

Once mass-produced images became widely available the 19th century market for folk art paintings shrank greatly. People suddenly demanded life-like attributes such as perspective and foreshortening, neither of which folk artists were skilled at producing.

As the imagination and technical capability of folk artists developed, some inevitably crossed the line between naïve limner and accomplished and accepted artist. Many would say that early works by L.S. Lowry can be considered folk art but once he had refined his techniques he became a revered fine art world figure. It is interesting to note that the Andras Kalman who created the British Folk Art Collection now at Compton Verney is the same Andras Kalman who was a major agent for Lowry's work.

Walter Greaves (1846-1930), an ex-Thames boatman, is considered by many to be a British folk artist. However it seems that his association with Whistler and other artists elevated his work out of this genre.

Schooner in St Ives Bay, Alfred Wallis (1855-1942) C7-16.

Alfred Wallis lived and worked in Cornwall all of his life. He came to painting late in life after an unremarkable career dealing in marine supplies. From his early seventies, then living in St Ives, he produced studies of nautical scenes 'for company'. They were sold to anyone who expressed an interest for just a few pence. He usually worked in ordinary household paint on scraps of card or board donated by friends and neighbours. This painting, in oil and pencil on card, is typical.

At top right is the Godrevy lighthouse and top left is Smeatons pier. Despite having his work brought to the attention of the 'outside world' in 1928 by artists Ben and Winifred Nicholson and Christopher Wood he died penniless, having saved just enough to avoid a pauper's grave. He now has a substantial worldwide following.

Festival of Britain wall hanging, Michael O'Connell, 1952. C7-05.
O'Connell was commissioned to produce this wall hanging for the Country Pavilion at the Festival of Britain. The finished work was 56 metres long and constructed on a backing of rayon hopsack. This image is of Yorkshire, the Grain Belt. The caption reads 'Across these wild chalk wolds are spread the large grain fields of Britain. Fields of wheat stand 500 acres broad and make good tractor country. The farm raises sheep and cattle too, for meat and milk and to keep the land in heart'.

Another relatively late-starter, Beryl Cook started painting in earnest at the age of 37 when she moved to Plymouth to run a theatrical boarding house with her husband John. She had previously worked as a showgirl and in the fashion industry. Her first exhibition in 1975 resulted in great public acclaim and her plumply cheeky paintings have been in demand ever since. She always managed to include humour while avoiding the potential dark side of some of her subjects which included sleazy clubs, gay bars and prostitutes, as well as more genteel bowls clubs and tea parties. Rubenesque bums and bosoms featured greatly.

Tango, Beryl Cook (1926-2008). C7-14

Boxing Match, Reginald (Reggie) Kray (1933-2000) C7-11
The infamous London character Reggie Kray painted this image of himself boxing,
watched by promoter Alex Steene.

There are many other contemporary artists who worked or work in the folk
art tradition. Some worthy of further study are Scottie Wilson (1891-1972),
Helen Bradbury (1900-1979), Julian Trevelyan (1910-1988), Tom Gentle-
man (1882-1966) and the celebrated Grayson Perry (1960-), some of whose
wonderful ceramics have a definite North Devon slipware feel.

Chapter 7 Cont'd - Signs

Trade sculptures and signs were used from the 16th century onwards to announce the business of the owner and to guide visitors before house numbering was introduced. They were a cut above painted board signs and had to be visually representative of the business conducted within for a largely innumerate and illiterate population. This form of advertisement for taverns can be traced back to the Romans who hung bunches of evergreen foliage outside inns. General-purpose painters whose main occupation was painting buildings and furniture for protection and preservation were called upon to produce most of these early signs. The majority were hung outside pubs (their stronghold still) and outside shops.

London citizens were first granted the general right to display signs on both business and private premises by Charles I in 1625. Inn signs or sculptures had been required by law since 1393. Most signs were of wood. Originally they were individually commissioned but then became available off-the-shelf in the 19th century. The biggest professional signs eventually spanned entire roads and by 1765 they had proliferated to such a degree that George III issued an Act saying that they should be drastically reduced. Air, light and safety returned to the streets.

Since the time of Henry V, sculptures of the two giants Gog and Magog have resided at the Guildhall, London and have been carried annually at the head of the Lord Mayors Show. These figures date back into English folklore of the Middle Ages and as they have disintegrated over time the original folk art versions have been replaced with more and more refined carvings.

Shops used a huge variety of both painted signboards and sculptural models to reflect the goods or services on offer – a giant key for a locksmith, a painted fish for a fishmonger, a gilded arm and hammer for a goldsmith, a large boot for a cobbler and so on. Some associations originally well-understood now seem obscure – an anchor for a printer and a grasshopper for a tea trader for example.

Lion Trade Sign c. 1750. In oak with
traces of the original gilt paint. 48 cms.
C7-03.

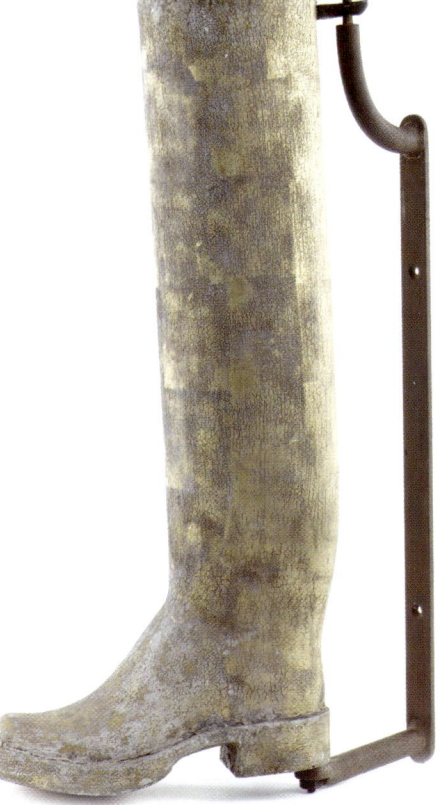

Early 20th century carved oak pipe tobacconist's
sign. 40 cms. C7-04.

An early 19th century
bootmakers sign.
C7-12.

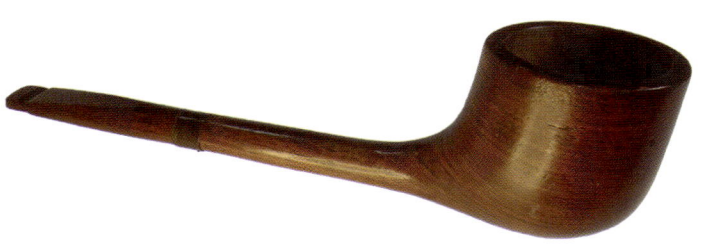

Copper and gilt Golden Fleece that would have hung outside a woollen drapers shop in the late 19th century. 68.8 cms C7-17.

Wooden model or diorama of a butchers shop c.1900. 61.5 cms. Possibly made by the butcher himself, it would have been displayed in his window out of shop hours to show the products he offered. C7-17.

20th century diorama depicting a country cottage from around 1910 at approximately 1:12 scale. 45 cms. C7-04.

In the early 21st century the majority of pub signs are, sadly, painted sign boards rather than representative sculptures. This was not the case in previous centuries.

Carved wooden sign for The Swan pub, 18th century.
101.3 cms C7-17.

The Boars Head pub sign, carved and painted wood,19th century.
90.7 cms. C7-17.

Sign outside the "Crown and Anchor," Shoreham

Pub sign for the Crown
and Anchor in Shoreham.
C7-04.

Pub sign for the Sportsman's
Call in King Street, Brighton.
C7-04.

Littlehampton pub sign. C7-04.

This is an area where amateur 17th and 18th century folk art sometimes became a full-time profession. A carver making one or two signs for family or friends would develop this into a business that would itself have been later expanded to produce ships figureheads and fairground carousel animals in the 19th century. Carvers previously employed on ships moved naturally to making fairground rides as iron hulls came in. Occasionally ships figureheads were reused as inn signs when they had outlived their original purpose.

'Turk' ships figurehead c.1850. 124 cms.
Carved and painted figureheads such as this were displayed on the prows of British ships from the early 16th century onwards. C7-18.

Figurehead from H.M.S. Elizabeth, now at Flimwell

Ships figurehead from HMS Elizabeth. It dates from the 19th century when popularity of these carvings reached its height. C7-04.

Figurehead of the barque "Arbutus," built 1863 at the Shoreham Canal ship yard (now Courtenay and Birket) for Jenkins and Co. of London. Subsequently she was purchased by R H Penney of Southwick and became one of his fleet of ships.
The figure is holding in her hand an Arbutus, sometimes known as the Strawberry tree on account of the similarity of its fruit.

Presented to the Marplins Museum by Mr A G W Penney.

Pair of painted fairground panels of bare knuckle fighters, one inscribed 'Iago Black' and dated '1854', the other 'Tom Sayers' and dated '1852'.
Tom Sayers (1826-1865) was a well-known pugilist who lost only one of his sixteen bouts. One of his fights, against Harry Paulson in 1856, lasted for 3 hours and 8 minutes (109 rounds).
172 cms. C7-12.

Individuality of design can still be found today, this half-relief soldier advertises the Valiant Soldier in Watchet, Somerset. C7-04.

One sign that has survived, although in diminishing numbers, is the Three Balls of the pawnbrokers shop. Pawnbroking was reputedly started in 1462 by Franciscan friars in Italy where the Three Balls (originally painted blue) were the symbol of the powerful Medici banking family. The song *Pop Goes the Weasel* refers to pawning (popping) a coat (weasel .... weasel and stoat ... coat).

There are still a few red and white striped barber's pole signs to be found in Britain. This design dates back to a service no longer offered in the 21st century. The customer would grasp a pole so that their veins showed and they were bled until they fainted. The bloodied bandages were hung out to dry from a pole outside the shop hence the sign.

Chapter 7 Cont'd - Sculptures

The two major mediums that must be considered for folk art sculptures are wood and stone. Generally speaking, folk art sculpture exhibits a lack of high quality surface finish when compared with fine art work. In interpretation it is direct and bold and rarely subtle. In some ways it is surprising that few folk art sculptors chose to work in stone, its structure makes it generally easier to carve than wood because no account has to be taken of grain and it can be cut in any direction fairly easily. Perhaps the need to handle and deal with wood in their day-to-day lives explains its predominance.

Sheela-na-Gig from Kilpeck Church in Herefordshire, c. 1140. C7-15.

Sheela-na-Gig figures can be found on several Norman/Romanesque English and Irish churches. The purpose behind the startling image of a woman squatting and exposing her genitals is obscure but is thought to date back to Celtic Pagan myths. Another theory is that the carver decided to go slightly off-message to produce an exhibitionist joke.
In any event this is a fine example of 'rude' folk art.

Corbel also from Kilpeck Church c. 1140. It appears to be an early version of the Green Man, a design which proliferated in the 19th and 20th centuries. The church originally had a row of 89 such images, some now missing. Their primary purpose was probably to impart moral messages but they must surely have been created to entertain as well. C7-15.

There are a few early carved stone pub signs still in existence and fewer one-off sculptures but the largest group of surviving folk art sculptures by far are the decorated gravestones in our churchyards. Skilled professional carvers used stone, slate, marble and granite to produce memorial tablets for those who could afford them. As well as symbols of death and time passed – hourglasses, skulls, cherubs and scythes – the stone would often indicate the profession of the deceased. Early gravestones often exhibit irregular spacing, quaint spelling mistakes and a general folk art sensibility; by the 19th century these 'errors' had been eradicated and the gravestone became a commercial and mostly for-mulaic product. This same development from local amateur to literate profes-sional took place with country milestones.

Some of the most keenly-collected folk art sculptures now (particularly in America) are those related to tobacconists. Life-sized models of Highlanders, Turks, Blackamoors and Jolly Jack Tars stood outside shops to advertise their presence and entice customers.

Tobacconist's Shop Figure in the form of a Highlander, late 18th century. In his left hand he car-ries a snuff mull and in his right a pinch of snuff. He is made of polychromed wood and would have stood on the counter of a tobacconist's shop advertising snuff.
The figure is based on the Old Pretender and many versions were produced of this size and also larger for use as an outdoor shop sign. Shops with a lower advertising budget would have displayed a simple representation of a roll of tobacco. C7-07.

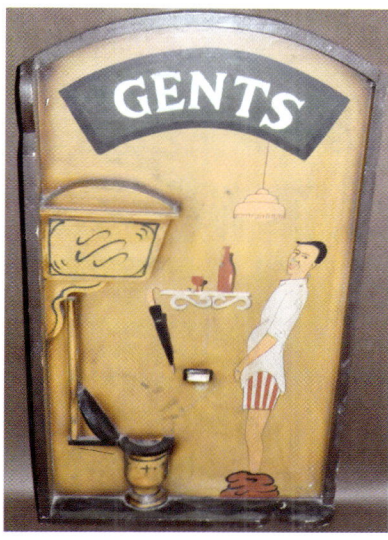

Pair of humorous lavatory signs constructed in relief, presumably for a public house in the mid-20th century.
69 cms. C7-04.

Decoy birds were made to attract real game birds towards waiting wildfowl hunters. Early decoys were largely made by the hunters themselves, they are rarely ornithologically accurate and are examples of amateur folk art. Commercial production of detail-perfect birds started in the 19th century and continued through to the last commercial operation c.1968. Although their form is strictly dictated by their function decoy birds are widely collected as folk art. Several species of birds were made as decoys. Ducks are by far the most common followed by geese, waders and pigeons.

Left, a decorative late 19th century decoy pigeon with painted feathers and glass eyes. Above, a working decoy of a similar date.
35 cms. C7-04.

A life-like silhouette was all that was needed for a decoy to be successful.

As previously noted, Punch and Judy glove puppets were commercially made and operated in fairground sideshows. The Punch and Judy show traces its roots to the 16th century Italian commedia dell'arte. Many other religious and secular puppets and marionettes were made between the 17th and 19th centuries. Some were intended for children as toys and others as adult entertainment. In 1738 Charlotte Charke opened a puppet theatre in London and commissioned a series of marionettes based on engravings of well-known public figures from a Mr Yeates. This lampooning of personalities by reproducing their likeness in wooden carvings was a popular pastime.

Judy glove puppet in carved and polychrome painted pine made in the late 19th century. She would have been part of a standard set including the Policeman, Crocodile and, of course, Punch. Her clothing and hat follow traditional designs.
58 cms. C7-07.

This saggy-breasted hag could possibly have been used as part of a Punch & Judy show in the 19th century. She does not exactly represent any of the normal Punch & Judy characters however, so it is also possible that she was intended to be positioned by a cottage door to ward off witches in the same way that 'spook signs', 'witches balls' and apotropaic symbols carved in ingle-nooks were intended to keep evil spirits and witches at bay. 53 cms. C7-04.

Late 19th century Clown chair, painted wood and plaster.
This chair was probably used as an attraction at a circus. Children would have sat and been scared by the grim expression on the clowns face.
107 cms. C7-04.

Early 19th century carved and painted hound C7-12.

Mid 19th century Highlander sign. 59 cms. C7-04.

Mid-19th century fairground leopard. 53 cms. C7-04.
He is appreciably smaller than many examples and is probably from
a childrens merry-go-round.

In the 19th and early 20th centuries there was a class of woodmen known as bodgers. Their primary occupation was to produce items of furniture ('hedge furniture' and Windsor chairs) using gathered wood but they sometimes made figures with no practical purpose other than as one-off sculptures. This figure of a traveller has been made from several pieces of wood, each chosen because of its natural shape. The man carries a staff and has a leather jacket and backpack. 32.5 cms. C7-04.

Whirligigs, made to spin in the wind, were really just whimsies with no real practical use. They were secured to garden posts and buildings for general amusement. The term comes from 'gig' meaning a whipping top and is applied to a variety of spinning or rotating toys. Some more complex examples included moving parts such as trotting horses and marching soldiers.

Three Whirligigs, all constructed of wood and metal and probably dating from the late 19th/early 20th century. C7-17.

Some of the most interesting amateur folk art sculpture was made from 'found' objects – scraps, butterflies, shards of pottery and so on.

These dogs made of interwoven strips from Players Navy Cut and Wills Woodbine cigarette packets date from c.1940. They were probably made by servicemen. Objects such as picture frames and hats were also made. 26 cms. C7-02.

20th century giraffe made of bottle caps (crown corks) 26 cms. C7-02.

Bible coverlet made by Catherine Harle from Spennymoor, County Durham c. 1895. The blocks of text contain biblical quotations, illustrations and musical scores. C8-07.

Chapter 8 - Textiles

Working with textiles, like woodworking, has always been within the reach of both amateur and professional makers. The materials needed were readily to-hand (either new or re-used) and the skills could be passed down from one generation to the next. Traditionally carried out by women, folk art textiles can be broadly divided into six categories : knitwear, lacework, quilting, sampler work, rug making and picture work. Materials used were generally wool, flax, cotton and silk.

Prior to the Industrial Revolution this was, literally, a cottage industry. Individuals or small groups would make garments or utility household items incorporating patterns that had usually been with them for generations. To a degree it was classless, done for entertainment by the middle classes and prompted by necessity for the lower classes. If encouragement were needed, clubs and organisations would be formed and government bodies such as the Rural Industries Bureau provided expertise to promote textile production as a source of additional income. As ever there were regional specialities; Honiton specialised in lace making, knitwear from Arran, Shetland and Fair Isle was very distinctive, parts of Northern England specialised in their own designs of 'progged' or hooked rugs and so on.

Many forms of decorated costume were and are geographically defined. In Marshfield on Boxing Day mummers wearing costumes made of strips of paper, the 'paper boys', parade through the village. In Lewes, bonfire societies organise the burning of dressed effigies on the 5th of November and the tradition of Morris Dancing is still alive in several areas, performed in traditional dress and accompanied by The Fool and The Hobby Horse. In 19th century fishing ports it was said that the pattern on a fisherman's knitted 'gansey' sweater was so distinctive that others could determine from which village he came or even to which family he belonged.

 Perhaps the most celebrated of the 'fancy dress' costumes are the Pearly Kings and Queens of the East End of London. In around 1875 a road sweeper named Henry Croft was named the Pearly King of Somerstown and the tradition seems to have grown amongst costermongers from then on. Their outfits are based on plain black suits and dresses smothered with pearl buttons in designs of Good Luck and Patriotism. There can be tens of thousands of buttons on a single outfit and they can weigh as much as thirty kilograms.

Pearly King and Queen from the early 20th century. C8-09

Tommy Cooper (and friend), Pearly King of St Pancras in the 1960s. C8-09

Trade banners started to appear in the 18th century and then proliferated from the mid-19th century to the early 20th century. They confirmed solidarity amongst groups of people belonging to the same trade union, profession or society. Many were professionally made. The London May Day parade in 1898 included four hundred different banners many of which had been made by a single company. The images incorporated can be traced back to several sources : mediaeval craft guilds, armorials, freemasonry, royalty, socialism and peace all played their part. Straightforward portrayals of tools or professions in progress were most popular. At the start of the 20th century the suffragette movement continued the tradition of marching banners to good effect. Eighteenth, nineteenth and twentieth century banners and flags were often a statement of pride in the quality of a particular guilds work or of sympathy with a particular cause.

Trade banner for Oldham Amalgamated Trades Council which was founded in 1857. It was professionally made at a banner maker's studio c.1900 C8-01

Tobacconist's apron in painted beige silk. It was worn by a committee member of the United Tobacconists in the Edinburgh Reform Jubilee Grand Procession in 1832. C8-02.

Flag of the Edinburgh Cabinet and Chairmaker's Society which was also carried at the 1832 Reform Jubilee Procession. The flag may date from earlier than 1832, the word REFORM has been added on the left for this procession. C8-02.

This wonderful Blue Bonnets Regiment banner is from Edinburgh and dates from c.1832. C8-02.

Banner for Keelby & Riby Pig Club which was founded by a Mr R King who died in 1896. Pig clubs were set up to help people supplement their diets by clubbing together to raise pigs for their own consumption. C8-03.

Smocks were a cotton or linen protective outer garment worn right up to the end of the 19th century. Heaviest use was in the countryside but town tradesmen such as butchers and tailors also used them. Workwear smocks were normally left plain but those intended as Sunday or Funeral Best were made of finer linens and decorated with embroidery and gathered smocking. Decoration often reflected rural pursuits – ploughs, flowers and sheaves of corn, or patriotism in one form or another. According to Gertrude Jekyll (R8-02) 'The smocking arose as a necessity of construction, for neither body nor sleeves were cut into shape …. this close gathering, though apparently chiefly ornamental, was of distinct utility, the much increased thickness giving protection to the back and chest, and whereas the whole garment would turn a surprising amount of wet, the smocked portions were almost impervious to rain'.

19th century Brown linen smock with bold front and shoulder patterns, probably from Norfolk. 196 cms. C8-05.

Young farm worker
wearing a Norfolk Slop
or Smock made c. 1870.
C8-05.

Patchwork quilting involves sewing together multiple pieces of material in order to achieve an overall decorative effect. Added warmth was achieved by the insertion of a piece of wool between material layers to improve insulation when used for a garment (perhaps a petticoat or waistcoat) or, the most popular use, a bedcover or coverlet. British quilting dates back to the Middle Ages when the technique was used to make light, warm and protective clothing sometimes worn under armour. The Victoria & Albert Museum has examples dating back to the 17th century.

Quilting was not necessarily a solitary pursuit; families and quilting clubs would cooperate on the production of larger, more complex pieces such as bible quilts. Creation of larger pieces could take several years.

A great advantage was that working class quilters could make economic use of old garments by cutting them up and reusing them in the same way that knitted pieces were often unravelled and re-made. Middle class hobbyists tended always to use new materials. It was one of the few folk art skills that benefited to a degree from the Industrial Revolution. Mass-produced printed cotton fabric from the mills of the Midlands and the North East added an affordable splash of colour to many quilts.

Brides quilts were a popular addition to the trousseau, they were worked by men and women and had a certain symbolic importance.

Silk patchwork coverlet dated 1718. This is one of the earliest known dated patchworks, the makers initials 'E.H.' are included in the design amongst flowers, animals, people and geometric designs. C8-06.

This rhyme is from a 19th century example :
At your quilting, maids don't dally
A maid who is quiltless at twenty-one
Never shall greet her bridal sun !

1850 coverlet commemo-
rating the loss of a child of
Edwin and Mary Bloom-
field. C8-06.

Cumbrian Triangles quilt
made by Bertha Mitchell
for her sister Elizabeth's
wedding in 1899. It was
subsequently used to
celebrate weddings for
another three generations
of the same family. C8-06.

Mariners compass coverlet made by Mary Dennis from Devon as part of her wedding dowry. Mary died in 1891 at the age of 92. C8-06.

Diamond mosaic coverlet made c. 1850 by one of Mary Cann's (nee Dennis) daughters. C8-06.

Samplers have been made in Britain from the 16th century right up to the present day. The earliest known dated example is in the Victoria and Albert Museum, London, and was made by Jane Bostocke in 1598 (R8-01). The earliest reference to their construction is in 1502 in the household accounts of Elizabeth of York. The name sampler comes from the old French word *essamplaire* meaning a sample or model (or possibly from the Latin *exemplum* with a similar meaning).

They were traditionally worked either by young girls (as young as six) as a proud demonstrations of their skills or by experienced embroiderers to provide reference pieces for others. Reference pieces might have been made by professional embroiderers but most samplers were worked by middle class girls and young women. It was looked upon as a wholesome and seemly occupation for gentle womenfolk. Pattern books were available and often followed but by far the most interesting examples resulted from the maker attempting to document her own life and experiences.

The two basic formats were *spot* samplers containing arrangements of individual motifs and *band* samplers with regular rows of border patterns. A standard practice sampler might include the girls name, age, the date, the alphabet in lower and upper case letters, Arabic numbers, a religious or moral text, perhaps a building or figure and several rows of patterns. More personal examples might include a family tree or a record of a birth or marriage. Many were completed as school exercises in the 19th century and included the

Sampler worked by Jean Swan at the age of 10, in 1752. It is in green and red woollen threads on a linen ground. C8-04.

name of the school. Variations on this theme were still being made in schools in the 1950s.

Some of the more academic samplers included map samplers (of a county, counties, England, Europe or the World) and almanac samplers which might provide all of the Sunday dates for the following 50 years. The accuracy of map samplers was often approximate.

A wide range of stitches was employed. A list published in 1688 of 'The School Mistris Terms Of Art For All Her Ways Of Sowing' detailed twenty-three different types. Some of these would have had basically the same structure but with variations of length or angle to achieve different effects. Outline patterns were often drawn or copied onto the ground fabric before being embroidered but care was taken to hide the pattern in the final work.

Sampler by Elizabeth Harryman, early 18th century. The texts portrayed are The Ten Commandments, The Creed and The Lords Prayer with Moses on one side and Aaron on the other. C8-04.

Sampler worked in coloured silks by Elizabeth Oxley in 1754, under the instruction of her teacher Mary Hewart. It depicts angels appearing to a shepherd, watched by a flock of sheep. C8-04.

A rare sampler depicting 'The African Slave' by
Esther Stewart, 1836. Slavery was not officially
abolished in Britain until 1838. C8-04.

Sampler by Hannah Woolfenden,
1841. The building is Bennett Street
Sunday School in Manchester. C8-04.

Sampler by Margaret Kerr aged 11, 1844. As the caption confirms, it was worked at Stewarton School in Scotland. C8-04.

Mid 19th century woolwork picture of HMS Minotaur and HMS Trafalgar. C8-10.

Charles II needlework casket c. 1665. This magnificent casket is included here because of its wonderfully naïve imagery which tells the biblical Story of Joseph. It is in coloured silks on an ivory silk ground with raised work and moss work. It contains letter compartments, ink wells and a silk purse. The purse is embroidered 'IEAN MORRIS 1660'. C8-08.

17th and 18th century English nutcrackers. 21 cms. C9-03.

Chapter 9 - Treen

For much folk art wood was the material of choice; it was freely available, easily worked and long-lasting. *Treen* has come to mean any wooden object, often turned, of size smaller than a small stool. It generally excludes items of furniture, transport objects such as wagons, and buildings. Treen has the huge advantage of acquiring patina and the knocks of use over the years. Combined with naïve design these signs of use provide a very tangible link with the past.

Apart from knives and chisels to whittle carve and shape, the main tool used to create treen was the lathe. This was initially a pole lathe which used a long pole as a return spring for a treadle which, via a cord attached to the end and wound round the work-piece, caused a reciprocal spin of the object. Subsequently lathes were powered by cranked handles and later by machine. Professional wood carvers needed a selection of between 100-300 different chisels to be able to handle all the nuances of curvature in a figure; amateurs this well-equipped would have been few and far between. The decoration on amateur work is often limited to chip-carving, which only employs straight lines, and simple text.

The evolution and scope of treen objects has been the subject of several books, most notably Edward Pinto's comprehensive and academic book *Treen and Other Wooden Bygones* published in 1969 and documenting his vast collection, now in the Birmingham Museum and Art Gallery.

Treen knitting sheath inscribed 'T S 1722' with chip-carved decoration. 22.5 cms. C9-03.

Stay busks were love tokens made to be worn by women in the front of a corset or other garment. They were normally made of carved and inscribed wood but also of bone and baleen. The earliest date back to Elizabethan times (R9-01). To *busk* is old English for to dress.

A minority of stay busks were made curved to improve the comfort of the wearer but most were straight. They range in size from around 25 cms to 38 cms.

Three professionally-made stay busks.
Top : baleen, Middle : box, Bottom : sycamore, curved, marked 'MV' '1747'.
36.3 cms. All 18th century. C9-03.

Amateur stay busk
marked 'M H' '1733'.
19 cms. C9-03.

Knitting sheaths, also known as knitting sticks or knitting bodkins, were used to improve the mechanics of knitting. They were used throughout Britain but seem to have a particular connection with the Yorkshire Dales. Tucked or clipped into a belt on the right-hand side of the body they held a thin needle located in the hole in the end. By using this needle to support the work-piece a hand was freed to throw the wool. Many plain utilitarian examples survive but they developed into love tokens given to a wife or lover and were highly decorated. They were also made of bone, brass and straw and despite their decoration most examples were still useable tools. A very small number plain sheathes were commercially produced by machine.

115

Knitting sheath early 19th
century, with caged balls
and ivory inlays. Marked
'ISa Foggin'.
15.5 cms. C9-03

Pair of 18th century children's
knitting sheaths. Top example
marked 'MV' and bottom
marked 'MW 1792'.
12.5 cms. C9-03.

Kit and Betty Metcalfe of
Gayle near Hawes knitting
using sheaths. C9-05.

Knitting sheath dated
1795
It was made entirely
from a single piece of
wood with the chain
links and moveable ball
being carefully revealed
by the carver.
31 cms. C9-03.

Professional
boxwood knitting
sheath dated 1860.
16 cms. C9-03.

This sheath is worthy of closer study. The business
end has a stylised pig ready to receive the knitting
needle in his mouth. The many images depicted
include a fox, the sun, the moon, a cockerel, flowers, human busts and stars.
Inside the hollowed-out 'cage' are several wooden
balls. This feature was a popular way of showing off
the carver's skill. The whole sheath is carved from
one piece of wood, including the caged balls. The
inscriptions include 'Victoria Albert', PLA 1860',
'PAULE GRUGE ORA PRO NOBIS'.

Snuffbox in the form
of a cow, fruitwood,
c. 1877. Inscribed on
a plaque 'Prize Heifer
1877 W.M.Gaskin'.
15 cms. C9-03.

Insect carved on an early
20th century Scouts tent
peg, presumably signify-
ing the Bee Troop.
31 cms. C9-03.

Apple corers are one of the earliest eating utensils known, dating back to pre-historic times. They were necessary in days when much of the population had lost their teeth and could not tackle an unpeeled apple. It was considered bad luck to share your corer, presumably for hygiene reasons. The examples that survive vary between plain function and highly decorated love tokens. Dated examples from the 17th century survive (R9-02). At one time it was thought that these utensils were for cheese tasting.

Late 18th century apple corer with two sets of caged balls. 16.5 cms. C9-03

Figural apple corer or scoop, inscribed 'A T' and dated 1757. C9-01.

Four 19th century pipe tampers. 9 cms. C9-03.

Pipe tampers were used to press down the burning tobacco in a clay or wooden pipe to ensure a good 'draw'.

Three sailors seam rubbers or liners, 18th century. 13 cms. C9-03

They were used to flatten the stitches on the joints on canvas sails and were made by the sailors who used them. They were made of hardwood, often lignum vitae.

Perhaps the most collected of treen folk art objects, love spoons were made by suitors as a love token for their intended bride. They often carry coded symbols of love, commitment and sincerity.

19th century Welsh love spoon with caged balls and initials 'A D'. C9-02.

Late 19th century love spoon with two bowls. The inscription, 'HAFOTY LLANRWST' signifies a dwelling (presumably the one pictured) in Llanrwst which is in the Conwy Valley, Snowdonia. 35 cms.   C9-03.

Pastry or biscuit mould dated '1876' in the form of a stylised fish. The design on the reverse side is of a costumed man.
20.3 cms. C9-03.

Combined Rattle, Doll and Hornbook c. 1800, made of turned and painted wood with dried peas to provide the 'rattle'. This is a very unusual combination of three normally separate objects. Horn books date back to medieval times and were used in schools as a teaching aid. The sheet of transparent horn allowed the educational text or scripture to be changed.
26.1 cms. C9-06.

Elder wood flower-head made by a Dorset Gypsy in 1952 during a spell of ill health that prevented him from selling wooden pegs. Attached to a stem, the flowers were sold door-to-door for 6d (2 ½ pence). C9-07.

A Housen used as decoration on top of a horse's collar. They were also made of leather with brass mountings but this 18th century example is of carved and painted wood. They are also known as Housings or Hounces.
51 cms. C9-07.

Professionally-made Georgian moneybox in the form of a brightly-painted garden cottage. 11.5 cms. C9-03.

Late 13th century misericord from Exeter cathedral (reproduction). C9-08.

Misericords were small shelves under folding church seats designed to give a degree of support to standing clergy during long prayers or sermons. Most are 14th or 15th century and they were sometimes used by carvers as an opportunity to introduce humour or fantasy creatures into the formal church setting. This one got the elephants feet wrong.

Chapter 9 - Metalware

The history of weathervanes goes back to at least the 9th century when the presence of a cockerel on church roofs symbolised Peter's betrayal of Christ. Over time this was combined with a vane indicating the wind direction and eventually the terms weathercock and weathervane became interchangeable. There is a cock at Ottery St Mary in Devon dating to c.1340.

They usually consist of a pivoted motif which rotates in the wind, plus arms indicating the wind direction. The motif was often a cock but many other designs exist – heraldic shields, patriotic emblems, birds and animals, hunting groups, blacksmiths at work and so on. The letters N,S,W &E were occasionally substituted. 'GDTK' (God Damn The Kaiser) was later replaced by 'GBTQ' (God Bless The Queen) on a weathervane in First World War Sussex.

There are records of a weathervane at Exeter's North Gate back as far as 1558. A version (possibly not the original vane) in the shape of a wyvern was moved to the quayside when the Gate was demolished in 1769. It was moved back to the North Gate in 1897 and in 2010 this modern version, an exact replica, was installed opposite the City Gate.

Wyvern weathervane – replica made
by silversmith Neil Bollen, Exeter.
C9-04

Moulded copper cock weathervane,
mid-19th century.
66 cms. C9-01.

Three 19th century brass West Country Friendly Society poleheads, 23 cms. C9-03
Each Friendly Society had a different polehead design – sometimes simple shapes such
as these and sometimes more elaborate depictions of animals , ships etc. Friendly Societies were setup to provide financial benefits such as funeral charges to working people
who contributed regularly to a common fund. They organised social events including
an annual feast for members. Several survive today. R9-03.

Brass comb rack in the shape of a crown c. 1893. 23 cms. C9-05.

These tidies were often made for their wives by colliery engineers. They were used to hold odds and ends – pens, pencils, matches etc. as well as combs. This one commemorates a fatal train crash near Thirsk in November 1892. It was made from the brass of the crashed engine.

Two iron blacksmith-made nutcrackers, 17th century. 11 cms. C9-03.

Nutcrackers can be dated to some degree by the size of nut they can accommodate. The smaller of these handmade examples could only handle a cobnut of small diameter. This places it well before the advent of larger cultivated nuts in the 20th century. Many early nutcrackers were of very plain form; these two are raised from the norm by the addition of lever finials and heart-shaped jaws.

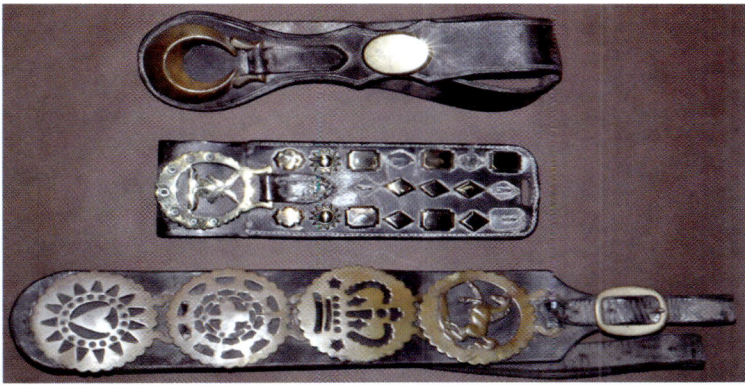

Three 19th century working horse brasses. 53 cms. C9-03.

Horse brasses have been around since the 18th century; they were used to brighten up the appearance of horses at country shows and on parade days Originally they were limited to a single brass on the forehead of the horse but around 1830 the fashion for multiple brasses started to appear. Reproduction brasses (stamped rather than cast) were made from the end of the 19th century when collectors started taking an interest.

Painted metal Firemark for the Bath Sun Company dating from the 19th century. The Bath Sun Company was established in 1771, subsequently merging with the London company in 1788. Fire insurance companies started to appear after the Great Fire of 1666. Each one had its own fire brigade which, in theory, would only respond if their Firemark was displayed on a burning building.
22.1 cms. C9-06.

Engraved silver love token made from a shilling coin blank. The obverse depicts a sailing ship with inscription 'MARY Yacht'. The reverse has a heart with Cupid's arrow and a horn of plenty. It is likely that sailor 'R Harvey' made the token for his sweetheart 'S.IRWIN'. The use of coins from farthings through to guineas as the basis for love tokens was common in the 18th and 19th centuries.
C9-09.

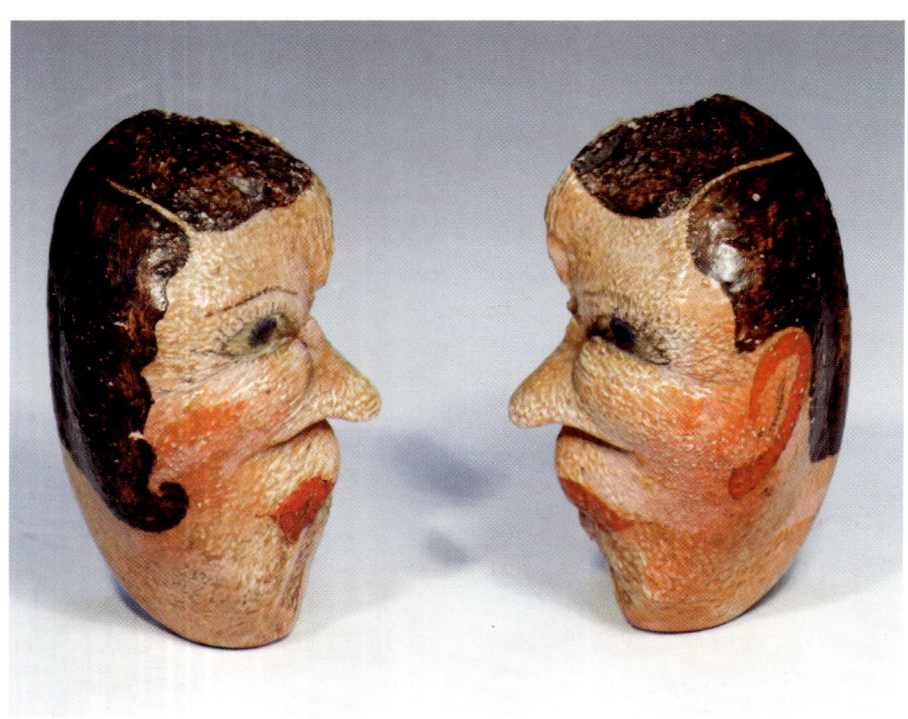

Pair of 19th century heads made from whales ear-
drums, probably sailor-made. 12.5 cms. C10-05.

Chapter 10 - Miscellaneous

This category of folk art is ideally placed at the end of the book because it comprises some of the most interesting and disparate items – a fitting finale to a summary of British folk art. As well as a wide range of decorative subjects the creators' ingenuity extended to using almost anything at hand as basic material.

The term Trench Art refers to decorative objects made for sale or as souvenirs by servicemen either while on active service or shortly thereafter. It has been made over a long period stretching from the Napoleonic wars when French prisoners-of-war made decorative items from discarded wood, straw and bones, right up to World War II. Wars produce much surplus material and with a few basic skills objects such as artillery shells could be turned into useful decorative items. It also provided something to occupy 'down' time when soldiers were well behind their own lines or recovering in field hospitals. It is likely that if the required piece of raw material was not available it would be 'liberated' from army stores and there must have been a degree of turning a blind eye by those in charge.

The variety of material is huge and includes : brasswork, embroidered pictures and postcards, lighters, cigarette cases, model airplanes and tanks, sweetheart jewellery and cushions, paper knives made from bullets, ashtrays, rings, bone guillotines, beadwork, straw marquetry, cribbage boards, mechanical toys, and canes. They often carried an inscription from the town they were made, perhaps 'Ypres' or 'Verdun' or simply 'Souvenir from France'.

Trench art vase made from an artillery shell, 1920s.
23 cms. C10-01.

Sailor-made sweetheart pincushion early 20th century. 18 cms. C10-01.

Toy WW II plane with hand-painted RAF roundels and the text 'IRIS'. 37 cms. C10-01.

Trench art brass ashtray. 14.5 cms. C10-01.

A strange little wooden trench art coffin. It has brass studs and the inscription 'MR NOD 41141 AGE 77 RIP S WILTSHIRE'. 10 cms. C10-01.

Toy rifle (probably a Lee Enfield, minus its magazine) with inscription 'MADE BY
PW 1902 St HELENA' 'TO HAROLD SUCKLEY FROM UNCLE CHARLIE'.
35.5 cms. C10-01.

Boody Pottery money box. Boody is a Northern England term for broken pottery
pieces or other similar small shiny objects. In the late 19th century there was a fashion
for collecting these discarded pieces and using them to decorate objects for the house.
In other parts of the country it was known as Shard Ware or Memory Ware.
24.4 cms. C10-03.

Traditionally straw dollies (or straw idols, kern maidens or babies) were made
from the last-harvested sheaf of corn as a fertility symbol or good luck token
for the next years harvest. They probably originated in the myth of Demeter
the goddess of corn. Regional design variations included Devon crosses and
Essex long twists. Their heyday was during the 19th century but there was
something of a revival for the 1951 Festival of Britain where Fred Mizen of
Essex exhibited a straw lion and a unicorn and they still feature in church
Harvest Festival celebrations in some parts of the country.

Two 20th century corn dollies in the shape of bells. 16 cms. C10-02.

A 1937 Worcestershire straw Cock that would have sat on the top of the rick or on a pole mount. 53.5 cms. C10-02.

Corn Dolly in the form of the Godess Ceres who protected the growing crop. 90 cms. C10-02.

Straw work model of a double-fronted house built on a wooden
frame. Late 19th / early 20th century. 12 cms. C10-01.

Folk art in bottles is variously known as God in a
Bottle, Patience Bottles, Crucifixion Bottles, Wish-
ing Well Bottles, Puzzle Bottles and most famil-
iarly Ship-in-a-Bottle. They are recorded from the
early 18th century and were often made by seamen
to be sold once they reached port. They are usually whimsies, made to illustrate the skill involved
in getting a seemingly too-large object into a rigid
bottle.

This example is from the early 20th century and
contains a wooden set of tools – spade, pickaxe,
saw, ladder and so on. It is in a Kia-Ora bottle (a
soft drink marketed by Coca-Cola in Britain from
1917 to the present day). Similar bottles exist with
the legend 'a replica of the tools used in making
the Dore and Chinley Railway Tunnel'.
25 cms. C10-01.

Folk art objects made solely of leather are relatively rare. This unusual 20th century sculptural relief was discovered in a pub in Durham; it represents a miner working a seam of coal. It is likely that its maker was in the business of making harnesses and the like for agricultural and pit ponies.
92 cms. C10-03.

Splint work objects fit together without the need for glue or nails. The notched pieces of wood snap together to form a rigid structure. These three examples are children's rattles from the mid-19th century. This type of work is known in England from the 18th century onwards. As well as practical objects such as baskets and boxes, decorative miniature chairs were a popular subject.
36 cms. C10-01.

Miniature splintwork chair
c 1900. 18.2 cms. C10-01.

Victorian/Edwardian wooden rolling pin with original applied paper decoration depicting rather pre-raphaelite women and flowers. This technique, called
decalcomania, was also used on glass and pottery items. 36 cms. C10-01.

Animal bone has always been widely used for tools and cooking utensils and as inlay for decorative pieces. This complete vertebra (probably the sixth vertebra of a Heavy Horse) has been painted to represent a preacher, probably John Wesley, in the act of delivering a sermon. It dates from the mid-19th century. It is not a unique piece, other very similar decorated bones have been found in the North of England. 13 cms. C10-01.

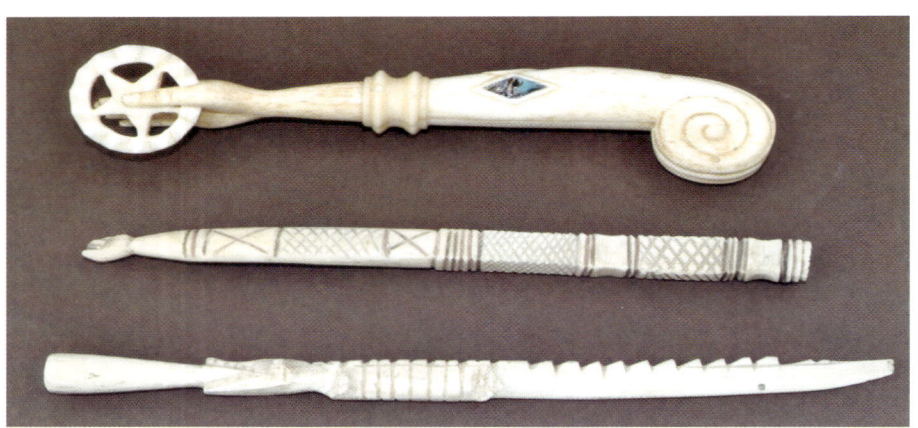

Three pieces of bone kitchenware. Top, a pastry crimper or 'jigger', below, two knitting sheaths (see chapter 9). All 19th century. 16 cms. C10-01.

Three whimsical hearth brushes which use the brush as the hair
or beard of a stylised face. Left and right are carved wood and the
middle brush is in beaten copper.
Early 20th century. 69 cms. C10-01.

A colliery miner from Roddymoor County Durham, decorating eggs, presumably for Easter celebrations. C10-03.

These beakers constructed from sections of horn date to c. 1800. They were decorated using a hot needle and depict rural scenes – coaches, buildings and country views.

Horn was a plentiful and therefore cheap resource and with the addition of a circular horn base plug it could be made watertight. 11.8 cms. C10-04.

As well as bargeware pottery (see Chapter 6) there is a class of highly decorated toleware items that was produced by and for canal users in the 19th and 20th centuries. Flowers, dogs, horses and the sailor's head from a Players cigarette advertisement sometimes feature, along with churches and other buildings. The overall designs are known as 'roses and castles'.

Anything that could be painted often was, including furniture, walls and tillers as well as buckets, scuttles and pans. C10-09.

Model of a mobile butcher's wagon, early 20th century. It was presumably made as a child's toy but the detail (including working brakes and steering) makes it possibly a display piece. The separate butchers block and tools are carried inside. 47 cms. C10-01.

Victorian domed glass wall decoration containing skeleton leaves - the skeletal structure that remains when a leaf has been dried. 22 cms. C10-01.

This book about Sussex folk art by S. Voules is a piece of folk art in its own right. It is handmade and contains original drawings, and photographs. Topics covered include ships figureheads, sailors work, tombstones and weathervanes.
28 cms. C10-01.

"What Picasso has achieved through the intellect..... many children are capable of achieving...."

Model cradle used as a bulb bowl. Made from the mud of Sandwich Haven by Ellen Cook, about 1930.

Miniature cradles decorated in slip were very popular in the past and were specially made to celebrate christenings or given as wedding presents. In the 19th century smaller ones were made as bulb bowls.

Pottery whistle in the form of a bird, found when demolishing the chimney of the Court Lodge, Udimore.

These birds were made with a whistle in the tail. They were often built into old farmhouse chimneys so that when the wind blew, the bird whistled which was thought to keep away evil spirits.

Carved bone staybusks from Hastings Museum.

INTRODUCTION

THE STUDY of popular art is perhaps of special interest to a teacher, for the lack of sophistication, intense sincerity and unconscious sense of pattern which are its predominant characteristics are also to be found in child art. A century ago even the most sincere child lovers would have scoffed at the term 'children's art' believing that true art could only be the outcome of years of labour on the part of highly skilled artists and craftsmen. To-day we are becoming more and more aware that the naive efforts of ordinary people, prompted by genuine emotion and an inborn desire for pattern and decoration about them in their everyday lives, can be a true and sincere form of art. What Picasso has achieved through the intellect, after years of study, many children and less cultured people are capable of achieving without conscious mental effort.

Popular art can be described simply

POPULAR ART IN SUSSEX

S. VOULES 1955 HIC FECIT

Glass rolling-pins - sailors' love tokens. (West Chiltington folk museum and Marplins Museum, Shoreham.)

Model of a church made entirely of feathers, quills and pins. From Potters Museum, Bramber—

An odd little tool, possibly used for trimming sealing wax. The increased presence of black and Asian people in Britain from the late 17th century onwards (one estimate of their number in 1800 is around 10,000 people) led to the inclusion of such images in folk art. Late 18th century.
7.5 Cms. C10-01.

This tiny *memento mori* is fashioned in wax and held inside half a walnut shell. *Memento mori* objects were sculptures or paintings intended to remind the owner of the fragility and short timescale of human life. Literally 'remember you will die'. This one was possibly intended to be worn on a chain.
Late 18th or early 19th century.
3.5 cms. C10-01.

Scrimshaw was the art of decorating the teeth, baleen and bones of whales, and the tusks of walruses. Images and inscriptions were scratch-carved into

the surface and then highlighted using candle soot, wax or ink. It was originally carried out by scrimshanders (often whalers) starting in the mid-to-late 18th century and continues today. Certifiably original early pieces are

highly valued, especially in the USA, but many fakes exist. (R10-02).

Maritime whale jawbone plaque. The panel top left is inscribed 'HM Sloop Acorn capturing the Spanish slaver Gabriel July 6th 1841'. Between 1807 (when Britain stopped trading slaves) and 1866 the Royal Navy captured more than 500 slave ships. Top right of the plaque are four Marines with the union flag. The central image is a fully rigged whaling ship with whaling boats hunting sperm whales in the foreground. 31.3 cms. C10-06.

19th century decorated sperm whale tooth showing a sailor with a straw hat in his left hand and a British ensign in his right hand. 'Cornelia' is inscribed on his shirt.
13.4 cms. C10-06.

Sperm whale tooth, decorated with a portrait of a woman holding her hands to her stomach on the other side of the tooth is inscribed 'CF 1840'.
10.8 cms. C10-06.

Whale jawbone plaque decorated with a milkmaid and farmyard scene.
7.1 cms. C10-06.

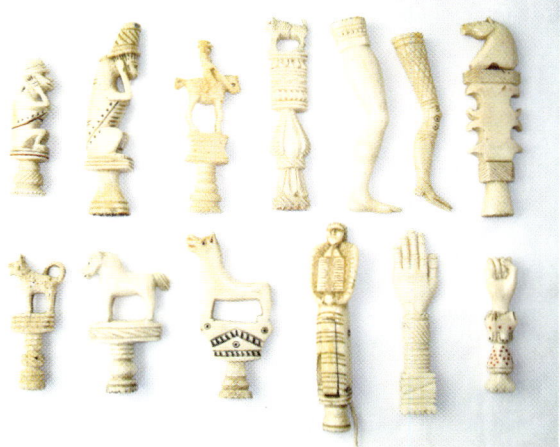

Early 19th century carved bone pipe tampers. 9 cms. C10-07.

Prisoner-of-war work was made by French Prisoners of War held in Britain during the Napoleonic Wars. They used any material to hand, often food bones (mostly beef or mutton) wood or bedding straw. Objects made included toys, boxes, bonnets, etui, corers and complex automatons of spinning jennies and guillotines. The objects were sold to supplement their hard prison life.

Early 19th century sailor (or possibly prisoner-of-war) toy. 7.2 cms. C10-07.

Early 19th century prisoner-of-war work decorated domino box. 12 cms. C10-07.

This is perhaps outside the definition of folk art but it is charming. From c.1815, it is a bill for 10s 10d (about 54 pence) from an illiterate brick-layer. Two men and one boy worked for three quarters of a day and used two hods of mortar. The crosses are signatures and the hanging figure signifies that the bill is settled. R10-01.

Some materials not included in detail in this book but worthy of mention in a folk art context are :

Chalk	-	prisoners of war sometimes made decorative carvings in chalk
Coal	-	miners carved good luck tokens such as shoes and boots from suitable pieces of fine-grain coal. Larger pieces such a tabletops and even full-sized furniture were also made.
Hair	-	watch chains, bracelets and rings were woven from either human or horse hair.
Slate	-	Welsh and Scottish miners, in particular, made small sculptural pieces of fish and animals and suites of miniature furniture comprising dressers, chairs, longcase clocks and fireplaces. Slate was also used for tombstones.

Black and white engraved advertising paper for
tobacconist William Gribble from Barnstaple,
Devon.
8 cms. C10-08.

Ockenden Manor, Cuckfield   Place Lane, Seaford
          Black Lion brewery, Brighton.

Chapter 11 - British Folk Art Collections

Museums

There are few collections of folk art in British museums, it often falls outside of their normal collecting policies. The only really dedicated resource is Compton Verney in Warwickshire.

There are several folk museums around the British Isles but the inclusion of folk in the name of a museum does not necessarily mean that folk art is held. Folk museums are much more likely to concentrate on the way of life of country people, emphasizing methods of farming and ways of living. Any folk art included is almost incidental. Those such as the North of England Open Museum at Beamish and the Milestones Living History Museum in Basingstoke have comprehensive collections of items related to rural life but few items which qualify as folk art – commercial or amateur. Many rural museums have individual examples of folk art or at best small collections but it is not a genre that is easy to find in public collections and they are often exhibited as curiosities rather than as cultural items. None of these museums differentiate between amateur and commercial folk art.

Some of the more important museums are :

Compton Verney Gallery

The Compton Verney gallery in Warwickshire houses the British Folk Art collection which the Peter Moores Foundation purchased from collector Andras Kalman in 1993 to ensure that it remained in the UK. It contains approximately 180 items.
Compton Verney also houses the Marx-Lambert Collection which was assembled by Enid Marx and Margaret Lambert who jointly authored two books on popular art. As well as their own designs this includes many pieces of folk art.

Victoria and Albert Museum

As a major repository of applied and decorative art the V&A might be expected to have significant folk art holdings, however this is not the case.
The museum was originally founded as a treasury of worldwide, not just British treasures. In its early years there was little space for folk art items. The closest it came was to include examples of Thomas Toft's magnificent slipware chargers amongst the medieval chalices and furniture. During the Arts & Crafts movement in the 1880s there was general nostalgia for English folk life and the V&A acquired a few folk art pieces. At the start of the 20th century Lady Dorothy Nevill's collection of Sussex ironwork was acquired by the museum. This included fire-dogs, firebacks, rush-holders, candlesticks and the like. The majority of these pieces were utilitarian rather than of artistic value but some firebacks do have folk art appeal. Much later, Barbara Jones (see Chapter 4) records that the V&A refused the gift of a roundabout.

A statement made on the opening of the new V&A building in 1909 confirmed that the museum would include 'the best work of English craft'; amateur craft was apparently not considered worthy however. As time progressed, their sphere of acquisition was widened to include the Victorian and Edwardian applied arts but the main thrust of their acquisition was (and is) in the academic and professional decorative arts – the artefacts of the wealthy rather than Everyman. In 1998 a study asking for visitors opinions of the planned British Galleries project did elicit several comments about the absence of objects related to the life of ordinary folk and their art but this doesn't seem to have had a discernable impact on acquisitions.

Museum of English Rural Life

This museum has recently moved from the campus of Reading University into central Reading. Its collections are heavily biased towards 'tools of the trade' such as pitchforks and pegs and it has several decorated wagons and some smaller folk art objects such as nutcrackers. In discussion with its curator, his view is that most folk art items were actually commercially produced and that true one-off folk art items are rarely found; these items are really outside of his collecting policy.

Horniman Museum

Frederick Horniman was an avid collector of European folk art and this museum's commitment to research in this area was stated in their acquisition policy statement of 2005. Their holdings cover folk art from around the world.

Pitt-Rivers Museum

The Pitt-Rivers worldwide collection is mainly ethnographic and archaeological but it does contain a number of interesting English folk art pieces in the English Objects collection.

Private Collections

It is difficult to assess the number of private collections that exist in Britain and there are now few UK auctions dedicated to folk art. Christies Oak sales often include some related pieces and examples occasionally turn up at other London and regional auction houses. This is in marked contrast to the United States where auction houses such as Garth's in Delaware, Thomaston in Maine and the New York majors hold regular sales of American (and some British) folk art. On 4th August 2007 North East Auctions in New Hampshire sold a large collection of mostly American folk art (The Dinah and Stephen Lefkowitz Folk Art Collection) - over 850 lots which grossed a total of $1.98M. There are few UK dealers specialising in folk art and some of these have a second string to their business. This seems to indicate a less than buoyant market but is also related to the rarity of true early pieces. Dealers in treen sometimes carry examples but significant pieces generally work their way through the trade directly to specialised collectors.

Government Organisations

Apart from those already noted, there is little support for, or interest in folk art by British government organisations.

The Arts Councils exists to promote the visual arts including : architecture, artist development, artists' moving image, crafts, learning and education, live art, new media, photography and public art. They comment that 'Folk Art cuts across some of these art forms and .... is also not specifically excluded from the art council's remit of working'. However, their interest is focused much more towards contemporary Arts than the past.

The Museums, Libraries and Archives Council (MLA) does not have any stated policy on folk art but its online database, Cornucopia, does provide many references to it in the collections that they support across the UK. Similarly, English Heritage does not have a defined policy on folk art.

Other Sources

In Britain in 2011 the most likely place to find contemporary folk art should be in the craft market; there are regular craft fairs around the country and craft stalls appear at County Shows, Village Shows and the like. A lot of the work produced under the craft banner is rather too painstakingly designed and sophisticated to qualify as folk art. As beautiful as some of this work is (woodworkers and ceramicists in particular are reaching great artistic heights) it does not generally belong in this book. It is careful, skilful and has artistic leanings.... but is somehow not folk art. If you do want to explore this later work the website of the Craft Council (www.craftscouncil.org.uk) is a good place to start. They estimate that there are currently 35,000 people producing craft work in the UK so there is a lot of work to explore.

Chapter 11 - Summary

No fixed rules can be applied when trying to qualify a piece as folk art or as something else; it is hard to define but easy to recognise when seen and handled. This can be frustrating in a world where silver carries definitive marks and porcelain carries maker's marks that can be quickly checked in reference books. Most 'antique' objects can be reasonably accurately identified by reference to other similar pieces which have confirmed attribution or provenance. Amateur folk art is different; the vast majority of pieces are unique and although many are dated, those that aren't often cannot always be directly compared to another object. This is part of their appeal, collectors look for something that expresses the enthusiasm, emotion and dedication of the original creator. Amateur folk artists were designer and maker in one and the greater the distance between these two disciplines the greater the degree of commerciality involved. In many cases commercial folk art moved towards 'one man one task'; this meant that the input of several individuals was necessary to produce an item which was then completely devoid of individuality.

In Britain we have no peasants so to a large degree we have no peasant art. Only 2% of the UK population are involved in farming, fishing, forestry and mining; the manufacturing and (overwhelmingly) services industries prevail. There is perhaps a tiny core of producers of amateur folk art active in Britain in the 21st century and very few of these artists use traditional hand-crafted methods of creating their art. The availability of professional tools (machine tools for production and software tools for design) means that a professional sheen is sought and usually achieved. Designs are very likely to come from a populist book or from the media generally. In the 18th and 19th centuries a large part of the population had not heard of the Renaissance artists; today everyone has been bombarded with images of works of art from all ages. The advance of modern communications has made it very hard for original folk art expression – untainted by fine art – to shine through.

The availability of instant visual gratification via television, the internet and the media generally, has meant that many fewer people are willing to attempt their own small expressions of art. It would be encouraging to think that different, electronic, methods of self-expression are replacing the older ways but this does not seem to be the case. Children still go through the delightful early years of naïvely drawing what they see around them but by their teenage years they have become consumers rather than creators. Perhaps the desire to decorate house interiors and to develop gardens has provided modern man with space for self-expression and replaced folk art. On the other hand globalised economies and MTV have a lot to answer for. Craftsmanship is not dead in Britain but a combination of craftsmanship and design uninfluenced by the strictures of fine art is rare.

In terms of nomenclature, the only alternative expression that might be widely agreed upon in the place of *folk art* is *non-academic art*. It is a lot less friendly, more negative and less evocative than folk art but it does cover all of the bases – naïve art, country art, folk art and so on.

In folk art one would expect artistic capability to be more highly valued than materials or craftsmanship. However craftsmanship and artistic interpretation can have a curiously inverse effect on the value of folk art. The more accomplished a piece, the less naïve it is and the less it is valued by many collectors. It is in the USA that the largest folk art collectors market exists. Prices there reach very high levels at auction, challenging prices for Fine Art at the highest level. In the UK the market is split between two groups. On one hand there are collectors interested in the curiosity, naïvety and cultural history of these items (the author amongst them). On the other hand there is a strong decorator and interior designer market.

Encouragingly, there does seem to have been something of a renaissance in the use of folk art imagery in early 21st century graphic illustration. It appears in book, poster, product and website designs. Perhaps this reflects a 'back to basics' response to an uncertain economic climate, or perhaps it is a reaction to the slick computer-driven-and-generated images that have become prevalent. In any event, it is a welcome development.

Website of Cakes and Ale Press by
Jonny Hannah. C11-01.

'Important' is a well-used word in the museum and auction house worlds
but it is very rarely applied to folk art objects. Given their rarity, charm and
relevance to Britain's social history perhaps it should be.

The last word is best left to the art critic Herbert Read (R12-01) : 'the object of
making the work of art is .... the thoroughly human everyday aim of *brightening things up a bit*'.

Very unusual carving of a woman sitting on a chamber pot. Late
18th century. 15 cms. C10-01.

Appendices

Appendix 1 - Credits

Throughout this book illustration credits are identified (Cn-nn) and are expanded upon here.

C1-01   Private Collection.
C1-02   Photography courtesy of The Potteries Museum & Art Gallery, Stoke-on-Trent.
C2-01   © Compton Verney. Photo by Prudence Cuming Associates.
C2-02   Reproduced by kind permission of Bonhams, New Bond St., London. © Bonhams.
C2-03   Private Collection.
C3-01   Photography courtesy of The Potteries Museum & Art Gallery, Stoke-on-Trent.
C3-02   Private Collection
C4-01   Private Collection
C4-02   By permission of the People's History Museum.
C5-01   Private Collection
C5-02   © Compton Verney. Photo by Prudence Cuming Associates.
C6-01   Photography courtesy of The Potteries Museum & Art Gallery, Stoke-on-Trent.
C6-02   ©Christie's Images Ltd 2010
C6-03   Reproduced by kind permission of Bonhams, New Bond St., London. © Bonhams.
C6-04   © Compton Verney. Photo by Prudence Cuming Associates.
C6-05   Images kindly supplied by Beamish Museum Limited, image copyright Beamish
         Museum Limited
C6-06   Private Collection
C6-07   Reproduced by kind permission of Tennants Auctioneers, North Yorkshire
C6-09   Reproduced by kind permission of Cliff Adkins (www.tobyjug.collecting.org.uk)
C7-01   © Compton Verney. Photo by Hugh Kelly.
C7-02   Images kindly supplied by Beamish Museum Limited, image copyright Beamish
         Museum Limited
C7-03   Denzil Grant Spring Exhibition 2011
C7-04   Private Collection
C7-05   Reproduced by kind permission of the Museum of English Rural Life, Reading
C7-07   © Birmingham Museums & Art Gallery
C7-11   Reproduced by kind permission of Gorringes Auction House, Lewes
C7-12   Reproduced by kind permission of Bonhams, New Bond St., London. © Bonhams.
C7-14   Girls Night Out CC Beryl Cook. Reproduced by permission of the Cook Estate
         c/o Rogers, Coleridge & White Ltd., 20 Powis Mews, London W11 1JN
C7-15   Reproduced by kind permission of John Harding and The Sheela Na Gig Project
C7-16   Reproduced by kind permission of Hayle Gallery, Cornwall
C7-17   © Compton Verney. Photo by Hugh Kelly.

Appendix 1 - Credits

C7-18   © Compton Verney. Photo by Prudence Cuming Associates.

C8-01   Reproduced by kind permission of Gallery Oldham.

C8-02   Reproduced by kind permission of The People's Story Edinburgh Museums & Galleries

C8-03   By permission of the People's History Museum.

C8-04   Reproduced by kind permission of Becky Scott of Witney Antiques, Witney, Oxfordshire

C8-05   Reproduced by kind permission of the Museum of English Rural Life, Reading

C8-06   Copyright The Quilters' Guild of the British Isles

C8-07   Copyright The Quilters' Guild of the British Isles and David and Charles

C8-08   Reproduced by kind permission of Christies Images Limited

C8-09   Reproduced by kind permission of The London Pearly Kings and Queens Society

C8-10   Reproduced by kind permission of Bonhams, New Bond St., London. © Bonhams.

C9-01   ©Christie's Images Ltd 2010

C9-02   Reproduced by kind permission of St. Fagans National History Museum, Wales

C9-03   Private Collection

C9-04   Reproduced by kind permission of Neil Bollen, Exeter

C9-05   Images kindly supplied by Beamish Museum Limited, image copyright Beamish Museum Limited

C9-06   © Birmingham Museums & Art Gallery

C9-07   Reproduced by kind permission of the Museum of English Rural Life, Reading

C9-08   Reproduced by kind permission of Philip Youle at Oakapple Designs Ltd.

C9-09   Image courtesy of Lockdale Coins Ltd.

C10-01   Private Collection

C10-02   Reproduced by kind permission of the Museum of English Rural Life, Reading

C10-03   Images kindly supplied by Beamish Museum Limited, image copyright Beamish Museum Limited

C10-04   © Compton Verney. Photo by Hugh Kelly.

C10-05   Reproduced by kind permission of Duke's Auctioneers, Dorchester, Dorset

C10-06   Reproduced by kind permission of Hull Museums

C10-07   Reproduced by kind permission of Rob Temple

C10-08   Courtesy, Abby Aldrich Rockefeller Folk Art Museum, Colonial Williamsburg Foundation, Williamsburg, Virginia

C10-09   Reproduced by kind permission of the London Canal Museum

C11-01   Reproduced by kind permission of Jonny Hannah (www.castorandpollux.co.uk/cakesandalepress/index.html)

Appendix 2 - References

Throughout this book References are identified (Rn-nn) and are expanded upon here.

R2-01   Art & Archaeology. XI. 185, 1921, dictionary.oed.com

R2-02   Folk-lore Journal, 1884, dictionary.oed.com

R2-03   *Observations on Popular Antiquities* by J Brand (see bibliography)

R2-04   For example, Thuro in *Primitives and Folk Art* (see bibliography) considers 'functional articles without applied decoration' as folk art

R2-05   Horton R, *From Child Art to Peoples Art*, Now-A-Days periodical, Spring 1947

R2-06   Lambert, M and Marx, E, *English Popular and Traditional Art* (see bibliography)

R2-07   Adam L, *Primitive Art*, (see bibliography)

R3-01   Mark Hearld, curator of The Magpie Eye, Scarborough Art Gallery, 2009

R3-02   *April Fool – Folk Art Fakes and Forgeries*, S Pennington, (see bibliography)

R4-01   OED, quoting Art and Archaeology magazine, USA, May 1921

R4-02   For example : John Smith, *The Art of Painting in Oyl*, 1723, William Halfpenny, *Perspective Made Easy*, London 1731. Robert Dossie, *The Handmaid To The Arts*, London 1764

R4-03   *Farm and Cottage Inventories of Mid-Essex 1635 to 1749*, , (see bibliography)

R4-04   *The History of Signboards*, 1866, Jacob Larwood, John Camden Hotten

R4-05   Higgs J W Y, *Folk Life : Collection & Classification*, The Museums Association, 1959

R4-06   Paine C, Assessment of Needs in the Museums and Galleries Sector – Steward ship, Heritage Lottery Fund and Re:Source, July 2000

R5-01   La Tene - The Swiss settlement where Celtic art originally developed c. 500 BC

R7-01   Antiques Magazine, USA, Folk Art Issue May 1950

R8-01   The Victoria & Albert Museum has a collection of over 700 samplers covering several hundred years

R8-02   *Old English Household Life* , Gertrude Jekyll (see bibliography)

R9-01   The Pinto collection in Birmingham has a stay busk dated 1660.

R9-02   The Pinto collection has an apple corer dated 1690 and a combined corer/nut cracker.

R9-03   The Museum of English Rural Life, Reading has a large collection of poleheads

R10-01   This is a reproduction, sourced from *Old English Household Life* by Gertrude Jekyll (see bibliography)

R10-02   Hull Museums have probably the largest collection of scrimshaw outside of the USA – over 350 examples.

R12-01   Read H, *The Meaning of Art* (see bibliography)

Appendix 3 - Bibliography

Adam L, *Primitive Art*, Cassell, 1963

Allan R, *Folk Art*, Beamish Museum Ltd, 2008

Anderson M, *Misericords*, King Penguin, 1956

Antiques Magazine - Folk Art Issue, New York, May 1950

Artmonsky R, *A Snapper up of Unconsidered Trifles, a Tribute to Barbara Jones*, Artmonsky Arts, 2008

Ayres, J, *Art of the People in America and Britain*, Corner House, 1986

Ayres, J, *British Folk Art*, Barrie & Jenkins, 1977

Ayres, J, *Two Hundred Years of English Naïve Art 1700-1900*, Art Services International, 1996

Banks S, *The Handicrafts of the Sailor*, David & Charles, 1974

Barker D, *Slipware*, Shire, 1993

Bennett G, *Folklore 95 Vol 106*, Folklore Society, 1995

Brand J, *Observations on Popular Antiquities*, Chatto & Windus, 1777/1888

Brears, P, *North Country Folk Art*, John Donald, 1989

Carrington, N, *Popular English Art*, King Penguin, 1945

Cooper, E, *People's Art: Working-Class Art 1750 to Present Day*, Mainstream Publishing, 1994

Deller, J & Kane, A, *Folk Archive*, Book Works, 2005

Evan-Thomas O, *Domestic Utensils of Wood*, Owen Evan-Thomas Ltd, 1932

Fletcher, G S, *Popular Art in England*, Harrap London, 1962

Folmsbee B, *A Little History of the Horn-book*, The Horn Book Inc., 1942

Gale M, *Alfred Wallis*, Tate Publishing, 2004

Hansen, H, *European Folk Art in Europe and the Americas*, McGraw-Hill, 1967

Harding M, *A Little Book of the Green Man*, Aurum Press, 2006

Harding M, *Gargoyles*, Aurum Press, 2006

Heal Sir A, *Sign Boards of Old London Shops*, Portman Books, 1988

Higgs J W Y, *Folk Life : Collection & Classification*, The Museums Association, 1963

Jekyll G, *Old English Household Life*, Batsford, 1925

Jobson A, *Household and Country Crafts*, Elek Books, 1953

Jones B, *The Unsophisticated Arts*, The Architectural Press, 1951

Klein G, *Arts et Traditions Populaires D'Alsace*, Alsatia, 1973

Laing L, *Later Celtic Art*, Shire, 1987

Lambert, M and Marx, E, *English Popular and Traditional Art*, Collins,

Appendix 3 - Bibliography

1946
Lambert, M and Marx, E, *English Popular Art*, Merlin Press, 1951
Lambeth M, *Corn Dollies*, Shire, 1974
Laver J, *Imagerie Populaire Anglaise*, Electa, 1976
Lewery A J, *Popular Art : Past and Present*, David & Charles,1992
Levi J, *Treen for the Table*, ACC, 1998
Lewis G, *A Collectors History of English Pottery*, ACC, 2004
Lewis P, *British Crafts : A Regional Guide to Crafts*, Sidgwick & Jackson,1983
Megaw R & V, *Early Celtic Art*. Shire, 1986
McCannon D, *From Folk Culture to Modern British*, Glyngwr Research Paper, 2009
Mockridge P & R, *Weathervanes*, Shire Books, 1997
Monson-Fitzjohn G, *Quaint Signs of Olde Inns*, Senate, 1994
Owen T, *Welsh Folk Customs*, Gomerian Press, 1968
Pacey P, *Family Art*, Polity Press, 1989
Peate, *National Museum of Wales, Exhibition Catalogue*, 1929
Peesch, R, *The Ornament in European Folk Art*, Alpine Fine Arts, 1983
Pennington P, *April Fool Folk Art Fakes and Forgeries*, Maine Antique Digest, 1988
Pinto E, *Treen and other Wooden Bygones,* Bell London, 1969
Pinto E, *Treen or Small Woodware*, Batsford, 1949
Read H, *The Grass Roots of Art*, Lindsay Drummond, 1947
Read H, *The Meaning of Art*, Pelican Books, 1931
Ridges B, *The Decoy Duck*, Dragon's World, 1988
Saunders N, *Trench Art*, Shire, 2002
Stead I M, *Celtic Art*, British Museum, 1996
Steer W, *Farm and Cottage Inventories of Mid-Sussex 1635 to 1749*, Phillimore, 1950
Thuro, *Primitives and Folk Art*, Collector Books, 1979
Turner W J, *British Craftsmanship,* Collins, 1958
Yallop J, *Magpies, Squirrels & Thieves*, Atlantic London, 2011
Young, R, *Folk Art*, Octopus, 1999

Appendix 4 - Folk Art Definitions

Formal definitions of folk art are rarely attempted, listed here are some which can be referenced.

The Oxford English Dictionary
No separate entry for Folk Art. Under Folk / comb : 'with the sense 'of, pertaining to, current or existing among, the people; traditional, of the common (local) people, esp. opp. sophisticated, cosmopolitan'.
First reference to 'Folk Art' – Volume XI, number 5 p185 of Art and Archaeology magazine, USA, May 1921.
Folk-craft : 'the making of traditional objects, usually by hand or by traditional methods; objects so made'.

The Shorter Oxford Dictionary
No separate entry for Folk Art. Under Folk / attrib & comb : 'folk art : with the sense of the (common) mass of people, traditional, popular'.

Britannica Concise Encyclopedia
'Art produced in a traditional fashion by peasants, seamen, country artisans, or tradespeople with no formal training, or by members of a social or ethnic group that has preserved its traditional culture. It is predominantly functional, typically produced by hand for use by the maker or by a small group or community. Paintings are usually incorporated as decorative features on clock faces, chests, chairs, and interior and exterior walls. Sculptural objects in wood, stone, and metal include toys, spoons, candlesticks, and religious items. Folk architecture may include public and residential buildings, such as eastern European wooden churches and U.S. frontier log cabins. Other examples of visual folk arts are woodcuts, scrimshaw, pottery, textiles, and traditional clothing'.

The Internet Free Dictionary
'Art originating among the common people of a nation or region and usually reflecting their traditional culture, especially everyday or festive items produced or decorated by unschooled artists'.

Museum of International Folk Art, Santa Fe, New Mexico
'the art of the everyday, rooted in traditions that come from community and culture, expresses cultural identity by conveying shared community values and aesthetics, encompasses a range of utilitarian and decorative media, including cloth, wood, paper, clay, metal and more. If traditional materials are inaccessible, new materials are often substituted, resulting in contemporary expressions of traditional folk art forms. It reflects traditional art forms of diverse community groups-ethnic, tribal, religious, occupational, geographical, age- or gender-based-who identify with each other and society at large. It

Appendix 4 - Folk Art Definitions

is made by individuals whose creative skills convey their community's authentic cultural identity, rather than an individual or idiosyncratic artistic identity'

Answers.Com website
'Art originating among the common people of a nation or region and usually reflecting their traditional culture, especially everyday or festive items produced or decorated by unschooled artists'.

Ethnic and Tourist Arts: Cultural Expressions from the Fourth World, Graburn, NHH (1976), University of California Press, Berkeley
'Art produced by the 'lower classes' of complex societies'.

Appendix 5 - Related Terms

Folk art and related objects are known by various different terms world-wide. Here are some of the more common ones.

Art Brut	French term meaning Raw Art coined by Jean Dubuffet (1901-1985), see Outsider Art
Country Art	Generally synonymous with Folk Art
Country Craft	Generally synonymous with Folk Art, although this term seems to be used more lightly
Family Art	Folk Art produced in a family environment, often containing personal family references
Folk Craft / Folkcraft	Generally synonymous with Folk Art but used more to describe the process than the end product
Naïve Art	Generally synonymous with Folk Art but more especially applied to pictures
Peasant Art	Generally synonymous with Folk Art
Popular Art	Generally synonymous with Folk Art but perhaps with a wider definition encompassing commercial products as well as more personal items
Primitive Art	Generally recognised as Folk Art originating in Africa and Oceania, often produced by full-time professional artists creating works (painting, sculpture) depicting religious, fertility, mythological and animal themes. Britain does not have this tradition to any great extent
Roadside Art	An American term meaning that which can be seen through the window of a passing car – billboards, shop signs and suchlike

Appendix 5 - Related Terms

Shaker Art	An American term for pieces produced by the Shaker community in New England, USA, particularly vernacular wooden furniture
Tramp Art	An American term originally meaning Folk Art produced by travellers and hobos but more recently adopted by the fashion world to mean shabby chic and faux riche decorating items
Outsider Art	Term coined by Roger Cardinal in 1972 meaning art produced by the mentally disturbed or deeply eccentric. Well-established artists such as Kandinsky and Klee are sometimes included in this genre as is the Scottish Folk Art painter, Scottie Wilson (1891-1972).
Vernacular Art	Used in *The Unsophisticated Arts* (ibid) to refer to machine-produced folk art
Yard Art	An American term, not much used in Britain, for one-off monuments and sculptures in peoples gardens/yards

Appendix 6 - Contributors

Bob Mills would like to thank the following people for their invaluable assistance and advice during the writing of this book :

Proofreading : Sue Mills, Melanie White and Sandra Wickens

Photography : Rick Ayres and Kate Mills

Illustrations and technical advice : Kate Mills and Sarah Mills

Cover design : Sarah Mills

Appendix 7 - Author

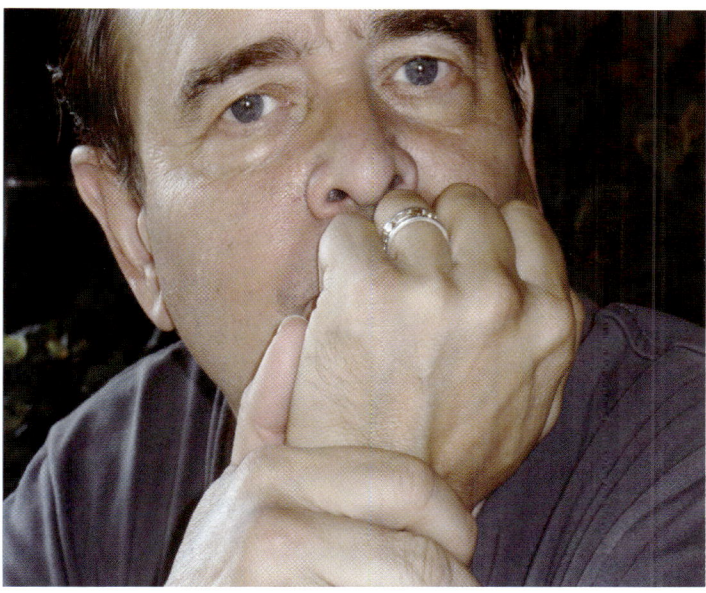

Bob Mills (BA Hons) is a UK-based collector of British Folk and Naïve art with an interest in treen items and early nutcrackers in particular. He has a degree in the History and Collecting of Antiques from Southampton Solent University.

He is also the author of Nutcrackers (ISBN 9780747805236) published by Shire Books, www.shirebooks.co.uk.

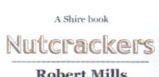

He would be interested to enter into discussions about British folk art or related subjects and can be contacted through his website :

www.britishfolkart.org.uk (email **mail@britishfolkart.org.uk**).

His companion website, **www.nutcrackers.org.uk**, is dedicated to collecting nutcrackers.